CLANDON
PARK

Surrey

THE NATIONAL TRUST

Acknowledgements

This guidebook has been written by Sophie Chessum and Christopher Rowell. They are very grateful to Lord Onslow for permission to consult, and publish extracts from, his family's papers on deposit in the Surrey History Centre in Woking; and to Trinity College, Cambridge for allowing access to the papers of Huia Onslow. They would also like to thank the following for their help in various ways: Trevor Adams, Caroline Blakiston, Peter Brears, Sean Buick, Rachel Campbell, John Cornforth, Martin Drury, Anthony du Boulay, Giles Ellwood, Dai Evans, Mrs Ivo Forde, Katie Fretwell, Alan Gallop, Julie Garner, Brian Godfrey, St John Gore, Terry Gough, John Hardy, Ruth Harrison, Catherine Hassall, Simon Jervis, Tim Knox, Alastair Laing, Mary Lambell, Dr Peter Le Fevre, Allyson McDermott, Judith Mills, Richard Peats, Mark Purcell, the Surrey Gardens Trust and Maurice Tomlin; and the house staff at Clandon Park, in particular James Doody and Helen Webb.

Illustrations: Blakiston family pp. 84, 85, 87; British Museum, Dept. of Prints and Drawings p. 71; Country Life Picture Library pp. 11, 13, 18, 48, 64; National Trust pp. 74, 90; National Trust Photographic Library pp. 34, 38; NTPL/Oliver Benn p. 60; NTPL/John Hammond pp. 26, 40, 43, 45, 53, 54, 55, 56, 57, 69, 70, 73, 75, 77, 81, 89; NTPL/Nadia Mackenzie front cover, pp. 1, 4, 7, 8, 10, 12, 14, 15, 17, 19, 21, 22, 24, 27 (top and bottom), 29, 31, 33, 35 (top and bottom), 37, 41, 65, 86, 88, 92, 94, back cover; NTPL/Nick Meers pp. 5, 51, 62; NTPL/Erik Pelham pp. 25, 58, 59; NTPL/Ian Shaw pp. 50, 67; courtesy of Lord Onslow pp. 46, 79, 80, 83; © Board of Trustees of the National Museums Liverpool (Walker Art Gallery) p. 76.

High-quality prints from the extensive and unique collections of the National Trust Photo Library are available at www.ntprints.com

ISBN 978-1-84359-012-5

Revised 2007, 2010

Published by National Trust (Enterprises) Ltd

If you would like to become a member or make a donation, please telephone 0870 458 4000; write to The National Trust, PO Box 39, Warrington WA5 7WD; or see our website at www.nationaltrust.org.uk

Designed by James Shurmer (4 10)

Printed by Acorn Press for National Trust (Enterprises) Ltd, Heelis, Kemble Drive, Swindon, Wilts SN2 2NA on Cocoon Silk made from 100% recycled paper

(*Front cover*) The dining table in the Speakers' Parlour set for dessert

(*Back cover*) The *Les Deux Pigeons* wallpaper, designed by Jean-Baptiste Réveillon, was put up in the Palladio Room in the 1780s

(*Overleaf*) The conductor, from J.J. Kaendler's Meissen monkey orchestra (Gubbay collection, Marble Hall Gallery)

CONTENTS

A PLACE FOR ENTERTAINING

On 27 May 1729 Frederick, Prince of Wales came to dine at Clandon Park. When the Prince left at seven that evening, he bowed to his host, the 2nd Lord Onslow, thanked him again, and, according to one witness, 'seemed well pleased with his entertainment'. Clandon had been built in the early 1720s by Lord Onslow for such occasions, and it has been welcoming visitors ever since.

Following his marriage to the Jamaican heiress Elizabeth Knight in 1708, the 2nd Lord Onslow was wealthy enough to build on this grand scale. He probably also wanted to celebrate his family's elevation to the peerage in 1716 with a suitably impressive and fashionable new house. His architect was the Venetian Giacomo Leoni, who had brought to England a first-hand knowledge of the Palladian villa style, which inspired Clandon and so many other early 18th-century country houses.

The exterior of Clandon is uncompromising and unadorned, but the interior with its virtuoso sculptural decoration is magnificent. The *stuccadore* Giuseppe Artari was responsible for the plaster ceilings, the most impressive of which is in the Marble Hall, where life-size figures threaten to fall

A Strasbourg faience tureen from the Gubbay collection

from their perches. The outstanding pair of over-mantel reliefs, carved in marble by John Michael Rysbrack with themes of hunting and dining, reflect Clandon Park's role as a place for entertaining. Regular guests would have included the Onslows' Whig supporters in Surrey, political cronies from London and fellow peers. An additional draw would have been the race meetings held on the Clandon estate at Merrow Down.

The Onslow family is unique in providing three Speakers for the House of Commons. The last of these, Arthur Onslow, who is known as the Great Speaker, presided in the Commons for 33 years and set a high standard of impartiality and honesty for his successors. The Onslow Speakers were commemorated by the Great Speaker's son, the 4th Lord Onslow, who created the Speakers' Parlour, adorned with portraits of the three Onslow holders of that office.

An Earldom was conferred on the 4th Lord Onslow in 1801 and he was succeeded by his frivolous son Tom, who is remembered for his skills as a carriage driver. After the 2nd Earl fell out with his son, Clandon lay empty from 1819 until 1876, when it was inherited by the 3rd Earl's great-nephew, Hillier.

During the late 19th century, the 4th Earl sensitively redecorated the house and remodelled the garden. The house and seven acres of garden were given to the National Trust by the 4th Earl's daughter, Gwendolen, Lady Iveagh, in 1956. In 1969–70 the leading interior designer John Fowler redecorated the house to accommodate the Gubbay bequest of furniture and porcelain, which came to Clandon in 1969. During redecoration, Fowler discovered rare 18th-century wallpaper schemes in the Green Damask Bedroom and Green Drawing Room. Today, the present Lord Onslow and his family live in a house in the park.

(Right) The south front

TOUR OF THE HOUSE

THE MARBLE HALL

One of the most dramatic entrance halls in England, the Marble Hall rises to the attics. The marble pavement is continued through the mahogany double doors to the Saloon beyond, and with these doors open, the whole width of the building is open to view, increasing the sense of grandeur. The (originally mahogany) doors in the corners also lead to marble-paved halls (three out of four survive), giving access to the rooms on all sides of the house, and to the two principal staircases and a servants' stair.

The Marble Hall was not only where guests were received, but also where large parties could be entertained. Dining-tables would have been placed here (two were listed in 1778) and in the adjacent Saloon to cater for particularly large numbers of guests. This tradition continued: in 1874, 110 people – including the then Duke of Newcastle – 'sat down' to lunch here. In good weather, external doors both in the Marble Hall and Saloon could be thrown open, revealing views of the garden and park, and allowing people to enter the garden. The west–east orientation ensured that the two adjacent rooms were full of light in morning and evening.

The white walls, Corinthian columns and the elaborate stucco ceiling – as well as the concept of such a vast space in the centre of the house – all derive from Italian villa architecture, but were also influenced by the English Palladian tradition. The Marble Hall is a 40-foot cube, like the Stone Hall at Houghton Hall, Norfolk, built in the 1720s and '30s for the then Prime Minister, Sir Robert Walpole. The Stone Hall also incorporated stucco by Artari and chimneypieces by Rysbrack. The interior decoration and furnishing at Houghton was orchestrated by William Kent (1685–1748), who may also have been involved at Clandon.

The antiquarian George Vertue on the Marble Hall, 21 August 1747: 'A Noble ascent in front [great] stone steps & balustrade – entring into a most noble and elegant Hall 40 foot high adornd with Marbles pillars carvings bass relievos by Rysbrake stuccos painting guildings &c most rich and Costly.'

WALLS AND CEILING

The stylised baron's coronets are in allusion to the barony of Onslow, conferred in 1716. They were altered after 1801 to reflect the family's earldom. The builder of Clandon was the 2nd Baron, whose wife, Elizabeth (née Knight), whom he married in 1708, brought a large Jamaican fortune into the family. The marble busts of blackamoors – between broken pediments over the central doorways – allude to her inheritance of plantations and slaves. These are the 'Two Marble Busts' listed here in 1778. They are, perhaps, by Giovanni Guelfi (active 1714–34).

The ceiling, with its Michelangelesque figures sprawling across the frieze, its varied imagery of war and peace, and its restlessly Baroque architectural forms, is attributed to Giuseppe Artari. It contrasts with the cool classicism of the wall elevations, with their two tiers of attached Corinthian columns, the open and blind windows and central niches. The imagery of the ceiling is eclectic, with no narrative scheme. The central circular relief is after Annibale Carracci and depicts *Hercules and Omphale* (the hero feminised by his love of Omphale, Queen of Lydia). In the corners of the ceiling are the four cardinal virtues: Justice (scales); Prudence (snakes); Fortitude (broken column); and Temperance (a bride). The profiles are of Roman Emperors or of generalised females.

The room was redecorated in 1968–71 by John Fowler, who uncovered the marbling of the columns and skirting boards in the belief that these elements were original. In fact, they were part of the 1870s redecoration by the 4th Earl, who recorded in 1879 that the columns 'had been rubbed plaster'.

The Marble Hall

CHIMNEYPIECES

The right-hand (south) chimneypiece is signed by John Michael Rysbrack (1694–1770), a Fleming trained in Antwerp who came to England about 1720. He certainly carved both overmantel reliefs of sacrificial scenes inspired by Antique models and was probably also responsible for the associated chimneypieces and framework (although these elements may be – as at Houghton – by another hand). The use of dark grey marble as a background to the overmantels is a subtle touch that increases the sense of depth, and draws attention to the pictorial qualities of the reliefs. The south chimneypiece is dedicated to Diana and the chase (hunting horns, boars' heads, etc.), the north chimneypiece to Bacchus, with garlands of vine-leaves and grapes.

The Marble Hall chimneypieces incorporate marble reliefs by Rysbrack

FURNITURE

The pair of marble-topped mahogany and rosewood side-tables on either side of the Saloon door are listed here in 1778, and were almost certainly made for the positions they still occupy (they fit exactly beneath the blind windows). The carved shells in the frieze and lion masks on the cabriole legs are typical of the style of William Kent. Hardwoods were preferred to giltwood because of their durability; the rooms beyond the Hall and Saloon would have been furnished more grandly in giltwood.

The hall-chairs (eight from a set of twelve) of Italian *sgabello* form are English, *c.*1730, and again were probably made for the room, as they appear in the 1778 inventory. In 1778 the only other pieces of furniture were 'two mahogany Dining Tables' (which could be used here, or carried to other rooms).

The four high-backed upholstered armchairs are Venetian, 17th-century, and are presumably connected with the 4th Earl's furnishing of the Marble Hall as a quasi-drawing room in the 1870s. This is also the date when *the Venetian wall-lanterns* and *the white and gold Italian altar candlesticks* were introduced to the room.

In 1778 the Marble Hall was lit by 'Four Bell Lamps with brass Branches and Burners' and four standard lamps ('Four others with brass Stands and Burners'). These were probably in the room from the start, as no provision was made within the stucco of the ceiling for a central chandelier, as at Houghton.

PICTURES

The pair of paintings of exotic birds, *An Ostrich* and *A Cassowary*, is by Francis Barlow (*c.*1626–1704), who was extensively employed in the 1660s at Pyrford Court, Surrey, which was bought in 1677 by Denzil Onslow (1640/1–1721), fifth son of the 1st Baronet (see p. 16 for biography and p. 36 for descriptions of his other pictures by Barlow, all of which came to Clandon in 1721). Such birds were rare in England in the 17th and early 18th centuries, being confined to royal or aristocratic menageries. It is unclear whether these two pictures were painted for Pyrford or for Clandon.

THE SALOON

Now hung with tapestries, and with a polychrome decorative scheme, the Saloon gives a very different impression from what was originally intended. As the entrance hall in the centre of the east front, it was paired with the Marble Hall. In the summer, both rooms could have been open to the garden, and the light could be allowed to stream in through the windows without damaging vulnerable textiles. The panelling was originally painted green, but was altered to frame the tapestries when they were hung here in 1879. The walls were decorated in blue in 1970 by John Fowler, who also uncovered the painted scheme of the ceiling by removing the whitewash applied in 1925–41. Fowler thought that he had thereby revealed the original early 18th-century ceiling decoration, but recent paint analysis has indicated that originally the stucco was painted plain white – as in all the other stucco-ceilinged rooms at Clandon. The present blues, terracotta and warm stone colours were in fact applied by the 4th Earl, as his diary for 1879 indicates. The contractor was Bargeman of Dorking, who also took down and remounted the tapestries.

CEILING

As in the Marble Hall, the stucco is attributed to Artari, and here is dedicated to images of the Greek deities in reliefs and medallions.

CHIMNEYPIECE

This is by Giacomo Leoni in black and white marble; the plaster overmantel framing a relief depicting Mars and Venus was presumably added by the Italian/Swiss *stuccadores*, as was the oval portrait relief above. The overmantel was redecorated in black and white by Fowler about 1970, but its original treatment may have been simpler. It was certainly painted white in a pre-1879 photo (white complementing the white marble frieze of the chimneypiece). A photograph of *c.*1910 shows the overmantel painted black, before it was again painted white. The black paint was probably part of the 4th Earl's 1879 decoration.

FURNISHINGS IN 1778

The 1778 inventory probably reflects the original furnishing of the room, at least in part. The walls were hung with 'Three Large Pictures of Fowls', which must be Barlow's paintings (now in the Stone Staircase and State Dining Room), originally executed for the hall at Pyrford Court and bequeathed to the 2nd Lord Onslow in 1721. Lord Onslow probably hung them in the Saloon (where they presumably remained until 1879).

The furniture was a mixture of mahogany and giltwood. Of the former, there were 'Two mahogany oblong Dining Tables, Ten mahogany Rail Back Elbow Chairs' and 'a mahogany Wine Cooler bound with brass'. This would all have been put to use for meals either here or elsewhere on this floor. The giltwood furniture consisted of three marble-topped tables. The 'Marble Slab of the beautiful veined Antique on a most elegant party gilt Frame' was probably placed on the wall opposite the fireplace, and may be the table now in the Green Drawing Room. The 'Two Marble Slabs on rich carved and gilt Frames' were probably either side of the Marble Hall door, given that no pier-glasses or tables were listed. The other contents were lamps ('Two Lanterns'), 'Two small Busts, Four large Shells' and 'a Set of the Cartoons after Raphael' (presumably a set of engravings after the famous Raphael cartoons for tapestries in the Royal Collection, on loan to the V & A).

PICTURES

The set of overdoors in matching gilt frames is presumably connected with the 'Five Portraits of the Pelham Family in rich carved and gilt Frames' listed in the State Bedroom in 1778. The Pelham portraits presumably came to Clandon by the marriage of the Duke of Newcastle's niece to the future 1st Earl of Onslow in 1753. All these portraits were reduced in height to fit the overdoor panels, when the panelling was again revealed (having been covered in fabric pre-1925) in 1958.

OVERDOORS

CLOCKWISE FROM LEFT OF CHIMNEYPIECE:

? After WILLIAM HOARE (?1707–92)
Thomas Pelham-Holles, 1st Duke of Newcastle-upon-Tyne (1693–1768)
Whig Prime Minister (1754–6 and 1757–62) and political mentor of the 1st Earl of Onslow, who married his niece. Owner of Claremont, Esher, where he laid out one of the most famous 18th-

The Saloon

century landscape gardens. Hoare's pastel portrait of the Duke is in the National Portrait Gallery.

ENGLISH, *c.*1728
Speaker Arthur Onslow (1691–1768)
The Great Speaker (for biography, see p. 69). He held the post from 1728 to 1761.

After WILLIAM HOARE (?1707–92)
Henry Pelham (1696–1754)
Younger brother of the Duke of Newcastle, he was Prime Minister from 1743 until his death. His garden at Esher Place, near the Duke's Claremont, was also laid out by Kent. The original is in the National Portrait Gallery.

ENGLISH, 17th-century
Thomas, Lord Pelham (?1650–1712)
Father of the Duke of Newcastle and Henry Pelham; Sussex landowner and loyal Whig supporter, created Lord Pelham in 1706.

TAPESTRIES

Part of a set of Mortlake tapestries of The Twelve Months, made in the 1640s. They hung in the Palladio Room in 1778, and in another drawing room from 1785 to 1879, when they were moved here. The original set was made in 1623 for the future Charles I at a cost of £500. It is now split between Windsor and Holyrood.

FURNITURE

The marble-topped table on a carved frame with lion's mask apron, and legs carved with a lion's mask and terminating in paw feet, is in the style of Kent, and is presumably original to the house. It had been thought that it was painted black in the 18th century, as part of its use for family lyings-in-state. Recent paint analysis reveals that the black is simply a result of the darkening of fake gilding.

The remaining furniture is from the Gubbay collection, comprising *two sets of four walnut chairs* (one of *c.*1710 with ivory inlay and original silk

The Saloon in 1925, when the overmantel was entirely painted black and before the mahogany doors had been overpainted

petit-point seats; the other – opposite the windows – is *c*.1720, upholstered in Soho tapestry). *The pair of marble-topped console tables* is possibly Irish *c*.1750; and *the pair of giltwood gesso pier-tables, c*.1730, is of the type associated with John Gumley (1691–1727) and James Moore (*c*.1670–1726), and is of the highest quality. They came from Kippax Park, Yorkshire.

THE GREEN DRAWING ROOM

Called the 'Green Drawing Room' in 1778, it was then hung with 'Party colored damask Hangings' *en suite* with the upholstery of the giltwood sofas and chairs. The curtains are described as 'rich green Lutestring Festoon Window Curtains lined with Tammy and elegantly fringed' so 'Party colored' must have meant green and another colour, probably in *brocatelle* (a heavy silk fabric). This almost certainly means that the hangings restored in 1879 by Williamson's of Guildford for the 4th Earl, previously in 'terrible condition, hanging in many places in ribbons', were the ones photographed by *Country Life* in 1925. They were still surviving

in 1969, when they had faded to a 'creamy yellow' and John Fowler pronounced them beyond 'pleasing decay'. He advised the Trust that once the room had been redecorated, and the Gubbay pieces introduced, then the 'original brocatelle will look forlorn and sad' and 'that splendid room will look disappointing and unattractively dreary and shabby'. When, soon afterwards, the *brocatelle* was taken down, the 1720s green wallpaper beneath was found to be in an almost perfect state of preservation. However, Fowler toned down the original glossy background of the block printed paper. He also regilded the room in what was assumed to be the 1778 treatment, added white highlights to the frieze (the ribbons) and green highlights to the ceiling (in Leoni's day the ceiling was pure white), painted and gilded the mahogany doors, and re-created (though using economical materials) the 1778 festoon curtains. The room was then arranged as a drawing room, incorporating pieces from Mrs Gubbay's collection.

CHIMNEYPIECE

The marble chimneypiece, given its similarities to those in the Marble Hall, seems to be of the 1720s, while the superstructure, with its pedimented over-

The Green Drawing Room

mantel in the style of John Flitcroft (1697–1769),
is an addition by the 3rd Lord Onslow in the 1730s
or '40s (the wallpaper survives behind it).

PICTURES

OVERDOOR:

Attributed to JAMES SEYMOUR (1702–52)
Harriers on the Merrow Downs near Clandon
Both the pack of harriers and the Whitsun race
meetings on the downs at Merrow were patronised
by the Onslow family. This shows the grandstand
where Frederick, Prince of Wales, was entertained
in 1729. His grandfather, George I, donated a 100
guinea plate, and the races continued to be popular
until they were eclipsed by Epsom and Ascot. The
last meeting took place in 1870. This picture was
probably commissioned by the 3rd Lord Onslow,
an enthusiastic patron of the Merrow races, where
his racehorses were often victorious, and where a
'great Cock-Match' followed the racing.

OVERMANTEL:

After GIOVANNI PAOLO PANINI (1690 or
1695–1764)
Roman Temple and Ruins

The Green Drawing Room in 1925, when the State Bed stood here

RIGHT OF CHIMNEYPIECE, ABOVE:

MARCO RICCI (1676–1730)
Wooded River Landscape
The nephew of Sebastiano Ricci, he specialised in landscapes, coming to England in 1710. From the Dutton collection at Hinton Ampner.

BELOW:

PETER VAN LERBERGHI (active *c.*1800)
A Wayside Chapel
Lerberghi painted Italian and Swiss landscapes influenced to some extent by Richard Wilson.

WEST WALL (OPPOSITE WINDOW), LEFT, ABOVE:

ENGLISH, 18th-century
George, 1st Earl of Onslow (1731–1814)
Son of the Great Speaker, whom he revered. A Whig politician, created Lord Cranley in 1776, he succeeded as 4th Lord Onslow later that year. In financial difficulties around 1780, he subsequently commissioned considerable alterations to Clandon and employed 'Capability' Brown to lay out the park. He was created Earl of Onslow in 1801. This anonymous portrait was possibly painted about the time he was elevated to the peerage in 1776. He married in 1753 Henrietta Shelley, niece of the 1st Duke of Newcastle, an alliance that ensured his political advancement.

LEFT, BELOW:

ENGLISH, 1813
Thomas, 2nd Earl of Onslow (1754–1827)
Succeeded his father, the 1st Earl, in 1814. In his youth, a friend of the future George IV, who often stayed at Clandon. He is best known for his expertise in carriage-driving.

CENTRE:

After Sir JOSHUA REYNOLDS, PRA (1723–92)
Susannah Gale, Lady Gardner (1749–1823)
This is a copy of Reynolds's portrait of 1764 in the National Gallery, Melbourne, Australia, and was made before the original was reduced in size. Susannah Gale was born in Jamaica, and in 1769 married there as her second husband Admiral, 1st Lord Gardner (1742–1809). The 3rd Lord Gardner's daughter, Florence, married the 4th Earl of Onslow in 1875. The horse pictures in the Stone Staircase by Ferneley were painted for the 3rd Lord Gardner.

RIGHT, ABOVE:

ENGLISH, *c.*1730–40
An Unknown Noblewoman
Traditionally said to be Henrietta Shelley, Countess of Onslow (1730/1–1802), this cannot be the case, as the portrait is too early in style (it is possibly by Pond, Knapton or Hoare). The ermine indicates nobility, and it is possible that this is one of Henrietta's aristocratic Pelham aunts.

RIGHT, BELOW:

ENGLISH, 1813
Charlotte Duncombe (née Hale), Countess of Onslow (1750/1–1819)
Pendant to the portrait of the 2nd Earl of Onslow hanging to the left, whom she married in 1783 as his second wife. Charlotte was an amiable character, much loved by her namesake, Queen Charlotte.

NORTH WALL, LEFT:

JOSEPH WRIGHT OF DERBY (1734–97)
The Rev. Henry Case Morewood
Signed and dated 1782
That this picture and the one adjacent should be pendants is somewhat surprising since, although the two sitters were to become husband and wife in 1793, when they were painted, he was plain Henry Case, the bachelor rector of Ladbroke, Warwickshire, and she was the wife of George Morewood of Alfreton Hall (d. 1792). On their marriage he took the name of Morewood. The two

pictures were transferred to the National Trust by the Treasury from the estate of Mr R. C. A. Palmer-Morewood in 1983.

RIGHT:

JOSEPH WRIGHT OF DERBY (1734–97)
Helen Goodwin, Mrs Morewood
Signed and dated 1782
The pendant to the above. These two portraits date from the beginning of the period when Wright was producing some of his best – and most naturalistic – likenesses. It is therefore a little incongruous that he still employs the somewhat old-fashioned convention of 'Van Dyck' dress, but it may reflect some role-playing in the slightly curious relationship of the sitters.

OVERDOOR:

Style of FRANCESCO ZUCCARELLI, RA (1702–88)
River Landscape
Italian painter of Rococo landscapes, influenced by Marco Ricci (cf Ricci's landscape to the right of the chimneypiece). A favourite painter of George III, many of his pictures are in the Royal Collection.

FURNITURE

Among the indigenous Onslow pieces of furniture are *the giltwood pier-glass, c.*1780, one of a series of such glasses (see descriptions in the Palladio Room, p. 20) and *giltwood pier-table, c.*1780 (reacquired in 1990 for Clandon) with an unusual painted leather top. Opposite the chimneypiece is an elaborate *glass, c.*1755 in the style of Matthias Lock (*c.*1710–65), the first Englishman to publish furniture designs in the full-blown Rococo style (1744). Beneath is *a green marble-topped side-table, c.*1730, in the style of William Kent, which may be one of the few surviving pieces of furniture from Leoni's Clandon and is probably the table described in 1778 in the Saloon. Opposite the windows is a Louis XVI *bureau à cylindre* (roll-top desk) of mahogany inlaid with ormolu. *The giltwood sconces* above are *c.*1765, the *chandelier, c.*1775, is possibly the 'Superb Cut Glass Lustre with Festoon Ornaments' listed here in 1778. The set of *giltwood armchairs* is *c.*1815.

The Gubbay pieces – here and elsewhere – tend to be on a smaller scale, such as *the mahogany and gilt kneehole writing-desk* (right of chimneypiece) in the manner of Kent (and supposedly from Wilton

A set of blue-glass and silver-mounted tea caddies in the Green Drawing Room

House, Wiltshire). The elaborate Rococo *mahogany fire-screen*, incorporating a contemporary needle-work panel, is very close to designs in Thomas Chippendale's *Director* (1754); *the walnut wing arm-chairs* covered in *gros-* and *petit-point* needlework, are remarkably well-preserved pieces of *c.*1720; in the centre of the room is a *finely carved mahogany tripod table* of *c.*1750 and *a stool, c.*1750.

CARPET

The extremely rare carpet, *c.*1760, the finest in Mrs Gubbay's bequest, was made in the Exeter factory of Claude Passavant (d. 1766), which was established after the closure of Peter Parisot's Fulham factory in 1755 (see p. 39 for a survival of that factory). Passavant's carpets – in imitation of the French Savonnerie style – were extremely expensive, and he was forced to close in 1761. Very few survive; one dated 1758 is at Petworth.

THE HUNTING ROOM

Called the 'Small Drawing Room' in 1778, it must have been so originally, serving as an ante-room to the bigger reception rooms on either side. It retains its original high 1720s dado panelling. The tapestries depicting hunting scenes give the room its present name, which is certainly as old as 1914. It is unclear when the tapestries were put up. Perhaps they are the 'Tapestry Hangings' listed in 1778, but they were certainly installed before 1870. In 1969 Fowler recorded that the walls were covered in 'modern' torn silk, and the 'nineteenth century wallpaper' beneath was 'too damaged to preserve' – hence the present hangings. The 1925 *Country Life* photographs show an elegant striped silk, gilt window pelmets hung with elaborate drapery, plain draw curtains and ruched festoon blinds. The present curtains were supplied by Fowler, *c.*1970.

CEILING

The plainness of the ceiling and the simplicity of the frieze and cornice, suggest that they are compara-tively recent in the style of the early 18th century. The 1778 inventory also makes no mention of a chandelier, although it is prominently allowed for in the present plasterwork.

The Hunting Room. Chinese porcelain birds on giltwood brackets from the Gubbay collection flank an English pier-glass and satinwood commode, both dating from the 1770s

CHIMNEYPIECE

The chimney breast – designed for the display of porcelain – is presumably part of the 1720s architec-ture, but the marble chimneypiece is probably of the 1780s, when the future 1st Earl of Onslow was making Neo-classical alterations.

FURNISHINGS IN 1778

The 'Tapestry Hangings' (possibly the present ones) were complemented by festoon curtains and uphol-stery of 'green silk damask'. The seat furniture consisted of 'party gilt Elbow Chairs' and a 'carved and gilt Sofa covered with party colored silk damask

Squab [cushions]'. A 'mahogany Pembroke table', various pictures including four portraits and a *garniture de cheminée* (a 'large blue and white Jar and four beakers') and a 'beautiful Needlework Carpet lined' completed the ensemble.

PICTURES

OVERDOOR (LEFT OF CHIMNEYPIECE):

Sir GODFREY KNELLER (1646/9–1723)
Denzil Onslow (1640/1–1721)
Signed and dated 1719
The fifth son of Sir Richard Onslow, 1st Bt, who bought Clandon in 1641. He is best known for his exquisite hospitality at his model estate at Pyrford, which was admired by the diarist John Evelyn. He married Sarah Foote (d. 1705), a considerable heiress, whose sister, Mary, married Denzil's elder brother, Sir Arthur Onslow, 2nd Bt.

OVERMANTEL:

DANIEL GARDNER (1750–1805)
Edward (?) Onslow (1758–1829), the 8th Viscount Fitzwilliam of Merrion (1752–1830) and the 11th Earl of Pembroke (1759–1827) playing Chess
Pastel
Set into a giltwood overmantel mirror of *c*.1775–80, a date that accords with the ages of the sitters. To the left is Lord Fitzwilliam; Lord Pembroke is standing with his arm on the shoulder of the third sitter, who is probably Edward Onslow, second son of the 1st Earl of Onslow. The picture – and its associated overmantel glass – was not listed in the 1778 inventory, which may indicate that it was painted soon afterwards. The tradition that the three friends fell out over the game, and that the stake was the Indian servant, has no evidence to support it. Indeed, it is unlikely that such a disagreement would have been commemorated in this way. Edward Onslow is connected with the story of a homosexual indiscretion in 1781, which caused him to settle in France. He soon found a French wife, and founded a dynasty of French Onslows.

OVERDOOR, EAST WALL:

ENGLISH, early 18th-century
Rose Bridges, Mrs Onslow (d. 1728)
Wife of Lieutenant-General Sir Richard Onslow, and sister of Ann, wife of the Great Speaker.

TAPESTRIES

The two tapestries, *The Hounds at Fault* and *The Chace,* depict hare hunting. They were presumably commissioned or acquired by the 2nd Lord Onslow, who maintained his own pack of harriers. Woven in Soho *c*.1730 and based on engravings (1726) by Baron (see p. 42) after designs by John Wootton (*c*.1678/82–1764), who was clearly influenced by French equivalents.

CERAMICS

The room is dominated by Mrs Gubbay's collection of 17th- and 18th-century Chinese birds, which are supported in part upon giltwood brackets *c*.1750–60 in the manner of Thomas Johnson (1714–*c*.1778).

FURNITURE

The pier-glass is English, *c*.1770, and is the most important Onslow piece of furniture in the room; beneath is *a semi-circular satinwood commode* inlaid with mulberry and fruitwood, *c*.1775, contemporary with *the pair of torchères with satinwood tops on giltwood bases.* Otherwise, the furniture is 18th-century, apart from *the late 17th-century Chinese lacquer cabinet supported upon a silvered gesso stand* of *c*.1690.

THE PALLADIO ROOM

This was the principal drawing room and may also occasionally have been used – possibly during the Prince of Wales's visit in 1729 – as a dining room. It has been known as the Palladio Room since at least 1747, when Vertue called it a 'spacious noble room'. It still has its Palladian proportions: its length is twice the height and 1½ times the width. Clearly, the room's original architecture was also distinctively Palladian and, as Vertue tells us, incorporated 'collums carvings ornamented richly'. This suggests an arrangement of attached columns (as in the Marble Hall) or pilasters, and indeed two pilasters still flank the central window, indicating that the room must have been similar to Leoni's Saloon (*c*.1730) at Lyme Park, Cheshire. In 1778 these 'collums' framed 'Four pieces of beautiful Tapestry as representing the productions of the Seasons' (now in the Saloon). There were also chimney-pieces at both ends of the room, rather than a single

The Palladio Room

central chimneypiece, as has been the case since the 1780s. These two chimneypieces were flanked by pairs of doorcases. In place of the present chimney-piece, there was a doorway, enclosed by a grander and higher broken pedimented doorcase, which via a marble hallway led into the Marble Hall. It was therefore possible to enter the Palladio Room – the grandest room in Leoni's Clandon – directly from the Marble Hall. Over the two chimneypieces at either end of the room hung – in 1778, and pre-sumably originally – the pair of full-length portraits of the 2nd Lord Onslow and his wife, still at either end of the room.

This arrangement was done away with by the 4th Lord Onslow in the 1780s, when the French *Les Deux Pigeons* wallpaper by Réveillon was put up, the Neo-classical marble chimneypiece was installed, and the furniture and furnishings replaced. The only decorative elements of the original room that remain are the stucco ceiling and the elaborate entablature.

In 1969 the wallpaper was taken down for repair, revealing the various alterations to the room described above. Fowler thought that the redecor-ation of the room in the 1780s complemented the colours of the new Réveillon wallpaper: the 'ceiling and dado were decorated in tones of pale blue-green, and white to match the paper. What is visible now [1969] is the coarse late nineteenth century interpretation of this colour scheme. The gilding dates from this later period.' There is, how-ever, no record of the 4th Earl redecorating this room in the 1870s. What is evident today is John Fowler's interpretation of the evidence for the 1780s scheme (although the colouring of the ceiling is his alone).

CEILING

By Artari, and, like all his ceilings, originally plain white. The winged female sphinxes, putti and medallions are in a more classical taste than the circular corner reliefs, which appear to have been taken from engravings.

CHIMNEYPIECE

The Neo-classical design is typical of the 1780s; the grate and fender are after a design by Robert Adam.

FURNISHINGS IN 1778

These consisted of a pair of 'magnificent Glass Frames with Ornaments most accurately carved richly gilt and burnished' above 'Circular' [ie semi-

When the wallpaper was taken down, the ghosts of the original fireplaces on the end walls were revealed

A ceiling roundel in the Palladio Room

circular] pier-tables 'finely painted with great Taste and highly finished in superb carved, gilt and burnished Frames'. The seat furniture was *en suite*: twelve 'carved gilt and japanned' 'Cabriolet Elbow Chairs' and two sofas, all covered in 'rich pea green silk Damask', which matched the festoon curtains and their 'covered Cornices'. Again, there was 'Wilton Carpet planned to the Floor' and for lighting 'Four cut [glass] Girandoles with Drops on mahogany Stands'.

PICTURES

WEST (FAR) WALL:

ENGLISH, early 18th-century
Elizabeth Knight, Lady Onslow (1692–1731)
She married the 2nd Lord Onslow in 1708. She was a great heiress (apparently worth £70,000), whose wealth largely derived from Jamaican trade and estates. Her money may have prompted the rebuilding of Clandon in the 1720s. She died of a 'raging distemper' at 39, regretted by all for her kindness: 'a woman of the truest goodness of mind and heart I ever knew', wrote Speaker Arthur

Onslow. This portrait appears to be a pendant to the full-length of her husband hanging opposite, but they may be by different painters (both unknown). The parcel gilt frames of the portraits of Lord and Lady Onslow are English, *c.*1730, and are presumably the originals.

LEFT OF CHIMNEYPIECE:

Attributed to BARTHOLOMEW DANDRIDGE (1691–*c.*1755)
The Lomax Family
Dandridge took over Kneller's old studio in 1731, and was considered by Vertue to be the ablest painter of such conversation-pieces. The portrait is on loan from Mr C. R. Grimes, a descendant of the sitters, and would appear to be about 1725 (as is the unusual mirrored frame).

RIGHT OF CHIMNEYPIECE:

Attributed to ARTHUR POND (1701–58)
Sarah (b. 1733) *and Helena* (b. 1735) *Selman and ?one of their Dighton cousins*
Probably the two daughters of Lister Selman (b. 1708) and his wife Sarah Mitford (d. 1738), who

were married in 1730. The third, smaller girl is probably one of their cousins, either Alice or Arabella Dighton. The Selmans were dyers and Turkey merchants. Lister Selman owned the manor house at Chalfont St Peter, Buckinghamshire. Bequeathed by Charlotte, Lady Bonham-Carter to the Trust.

EAST (NEAR) WALL:

ENGLISH, early 18th-century
Thomas, 2nd Lord Onslow (1679–1740)
Son of the 1st Lord Onslow, whom he succeeded in 1717. The first Governor of the Royal Exchange Assurance Corporation and a favourite of both King George I and II, he entertained Frederick, Prince of Wales in the new house at Clandon in 1729. Unfortunately, most of the furniture he commissioned was sold in the 1780s. Like his father, he was a staunch adherent of the Whig government of Sir Robert Walpole. The architectural background of this portrait is reminiscent of other full-lengths by the Swedish painter Hans Hysing, and the circular windows may allude to the similar windows in the Oak Staircase.

FURNITURE

The giltwood pier-glasses, overmantel glass and the torchères ornamented with rams' heads and snakes must all have been installed after the 4th Lord Onslow's alterations in the 1780s. *The pair of torchères* was originally part of a larger set. Slightly earlier, *c.*1770, are *the pair of giltwood sofas* and the *eight giltwood chairs*, which are English in the French style. Their contrasting yellow and pink upholstery is due to John Fowler, *c.*1970. A survival from Clandon around 1730 is the magnificent *giltwood marble-topped Kentian side-table*, and the large *bureau à cylindre*, which is French, *c.*1760.

From the Gubbay collection are *the two mahogany inlaid bombé commodes* beneath the pier-glasses attributed to Pierre Langlois, one of the leading cabinetmakers in London in the 1760s and '70s, who specialised in such commodes in the Louis XV and Louis XVI styles, inlaid with marquetry and with ormolu mounts. *The pianoforte*, 1814, by Broadwood is on loan from Mr Alan Rubin and is identical to the piano presented by Broadwood to Beethoven in 1817.

THE MORNING ROOM

In 1778 this was simply described as an 'Ante-room' between the Oak Staircase and Palladio Room. This presumably reflects its original function. The room was remodelled in the fashionable Neo-classical style of the later 18th century, presumably in the 1780s, when the Palladio Room was being altered by the 4th Lord Onslow. The plasterwork, woodwork and chimneypiece all date from this period (although the chimneypiece replaced a 1740s chimneypiece around 1970). It has been called the Morning Room since at least 1879, when the 4th Earl had it fitted up and decorated with 'Japanese tapestry to make a Smoking Room'. The room was redecorated and the curtains hung around 1970 by Fowler.

Behind the door to the left of the chimneypiece is the 'Measuring Cupboard', where the heights of Onslow children were recorded since 1781, when the five-year-old future 3rd Earl was measured.

PAST FURNISHINGS

In 1778, the room was furnished more plainly than the grander rooms beyond. Instead of silk, the festoon curtains were woollen – 'light coloured morine' – with 'scarlet Fringe Lines and Tassells'. The nine 'Cabriolet Party colored Chairs' had 'Carpet Seats brass nailed'. There was a giltwood overmantel glass, a 'Trou Madame Table', 'a fine toned Forte Piano' and a 'Guitar and Case'. The floor was covered with an 'India Cane mat lined'.

In contrast to this simple furniture, the 1899 inventory records an exotic compendium of lacquer and bamboo furniture, as well as easy chairs, suiting its masculine character as a smoking room.

PICTURES

NORTH (FAR) WALL, OVERDOOR:

ENGLISH, early 19th-century
Arthur, 3rd Earl of Onslow (1777–1870)
Son of the 2nd Earl, whom he succeeded in 1827, he married Mary Fludyer in 1818 (at about the time this portrait was painted), and was inconsolable after her early death in 1830. Their only son, Arthur, Viscount Cranley, died aged 36 in 1856, without a male heir, and this second bereavement further embittered the 3rd Earl. He continued to live at nearby Clandon Regis, even after his succession to

The marquetry games table, c.1770, in the Morning Room

the earldom, and following his wife's death, mainly at Richmond. Clandon was neglected, but not entirely given up. He apparently took against his great-nephew and heir, William Hillier Onslow, who was forced to buy back some of the contents of Clandon at the auction arranged in accordance with the 3rd Earl's Will.

RIGHT, ABOVE:

ENGLISH, 18th-century
Arthur Onslow, the Great Speaker (1691–1768)
A half-length variant of the full-length portrait in the Speakers' Parlour, depicting Onslow in Speaker's robes. For biography, see p. 69.

BELOW:

JOHANN ZOFFANY, RA (1733–1810)
The Mathew Family at Felix Hall
Mary (1730–1814) and Daniel Mathew (d. 1777) with five of their children in the park at Felix Hall, Kelvedon, Essex. This is one of Zoffany's earlier and most outstanding portrait groups, painted soon after his arrival in Britain in 1760. On loan from a descendant of the little boy seated on his mother's knee: George Mathew (1760–1846).

LEFT OF CHIMNEYPIECE:

JOHN RUSSELL, RA (1745–1806)
Mrs Nathaniel Hillier
Pastel, signed and dated 1801
Wife of Nathaniel Hillier opposite. Their second daughter, Susannah, married, in 1812, Thomas Onslow, second son of the 2nd Earl. The 4th Earl was their grandson. Russell, who was born in Guildford, portrayed several members of the Onslow family, and was a friend of the 1st Earl, with whom he discussed religion (Russell was a converted Methodist).

OVERMANTEL:

PHILIP DE LASZLO (1869–1937)
Violet Bampfylde, Countess of Onslow (1883–1954)
Signed and dated May 1929
Daughter of the 3rd Lord Poltimore, she married the 5th Earl in 1906. During the Great War, she ran Clandon as a military hospital. The National Trust has recently acquired a silver centrepiece presented to Lady Onslow in honour of her work. This is one of De Laszlo's best portraits, combining style with a degree of psychological penetration.

RIGHT OF CHIMNEYPIECE:

JOHN RUSSELL, RA (1745–1806)
Nathaniel Hillier (d.1883)
Pastel, signed and dated 1801
Merchant and collector of drawings. Of Stoke Park, Surrey, he was the great-grandfather of the 4th Earl of Onslow.

SOUTH (ONE WINDOW) WALL, LEFT, ABOVE:

JAMES BARRACLOUGH (d.1942)
Pamela, Countess of Onslow (1915–92)
Signed and dated 1939
Daughter of the 19th Viscount Dillon, she married the 6th Earl in 1936 and was divorced in 1962. She was the mother of the present (7th) Earl. Co-author of the first National Trust guidebook to Clandon, she regretted that the Trust's 1968–71 restoration by John Fowler made the house more of a monument than a family home.

RIGHT, BELOW:

FRENCH, c.1800
Marie-Rosalie de Bourdeilles de Brantôme, Mrs Edward Onslow (d.1842)
Married Edward Onslow (opposite) in 1783. They

lived in the Auvergne, founding a talented French branch of the family. Their most famous son was the composer George Onslow.

RIGHT, ABOVE:

DOROFIELD HARDY (active 1882–1920) after
JOHN COLLIER (1850–1934)
Lady Gwendolen Onslow, Countess of Iveagh
(1881–1966)
Daughter of the 4th Earl, she married in 1903 Rupert, 2nd Earl of Iveagh, the head of the Guinness brewing family, whose English seat was the opulent Elveden Hall, Suffolk. In 1956 she acquired Clandon, her childhood home, from her nephew, the 6th Earl, who had moved out several years before. She also bought the contents, the surrounding seven acres, and presented Clandon, with an endowment, to the National Trust.

LEFT, BELOW:

FRENCH, c.1800
Edward Onslow (1758–1829)
Third son of the 1st Earl, he was forced to flee to France after a homosexual scandal in 1781. In 1783 he married Marie-Rosalie de Bourdeilles de Brantôme (opposite), and he and their children became French citizens. Edward was imprisoned in

A Japanese porcelain duck from the Gubbay collection in the Morning Room

1789 during the Revolution, but was released due to his wife's efforts on his behalf.

WEST (TWO-WINDOW) WALL:

ENGLISH, c.1730–40
? A member of the Shelley Family
Pastel
Traditionally said to be Henrietta Shelley, wife of the 1st Earl, but this is impossible, as she was born in 1730/1. It could be one of her two elder sisters. Attributed to John Russell, it is more likely to be by another artist such as Pond, Knapton or Hoare.

FURNITURE

This room is almost entirely furnished with pieces from Mrs Gubbay's collection, including several more mid-18th-century giltwood brackets supporting Chinese and Japanese porcelain birds and fowl. *The painted and marquetry satinwood sécretaire bookcase* is filled with mid-18th-century English and continental porcelain. Flanking the chimneypiece is an important *pair of ormolu-mounted satinwood side-tables inlaid with marquetry medallions of a lion and a bull*, motifs similar to those on a pair of tables and a commode in the Lady Lever Art Gallery, Port Sunlight. They are attributed to the firm of John Mayhew (1736–1811) and William Ince (d. 1804).

In front of the chimneypiece is *a marquetry inlaid satinwood Pembroke table*, c.1770, of outstanding quality, fitted with a backgammon board. At the far (north) end of the room is *an elmwood and mahogany commode*, probably Dutch, c.1760, and *a satinwood lady's writing-table or bonheur-du-jour*, with rising fire-screens on the back and sides, English, c.1770. *The painted chairs with cane seats and backs*, c.1760, are from Lydiard Tregoze, Wiltshire, and were presented to Clandon by John Fowler.

RUG

The early 18th-century needlework rug incorporating an unidentified central coat of arms is part of Mrs Gubbay's collection.

CHANDELIER

The chandelier (c.1775, restored in the 19th century) is attributed to Christopher Haedy (active 1769–85), who had premises in London and Bath. Another chandelier, with Haedy's characteristic notched spires, is at Uppark.

THE OAK STAIRCASE

The oak balustrade is of the 1720s, and the decorative heraldic finials were made in Florence in 1881 for the 4th Earl. The circular windows on the landing were designed to light a hallway behind the staircase, which linked the Marble Hall and the Palladio Room until the 1780s. The framed panels in the plasterwork of the staircase walls are probably embellishments added by the 4th Earl in the 1880s. The present decoration is by John Fowler, *c.*1970.

PAST FURNISHINGS

In 1778 the furniture was predominantly practical, as this area was employed to store numerous tables for use elsewhere. There was also a mahogany 'dumb waiter' and 'A Large mahogany Linen Chest'. By the late 19th century, the Oak Staircase was cluttered by decorative arrangements of pictures, armour, antlers and firearms.

FURNITURE

The mahogany pedestal is essentially *c.*1730, but with 19th-century additions, and supports *a French marble bust of Napoleon*, probably from the 3rd Earl's collection of Napoleonic souvenirs (see p. 76).

Cross the Marble Hall and pass by the Stone Staircase to reach the Speakers' Parlour.

THE SPEAKERS' PARLOUR

This seems to have always been used as the everyday dining room (the Kitchen was immediately below). Hung with portraits of the Onslow Speakers from the beginning, the room is a celebration of parliamentary achievement and pride in ancestry. In 1747 Vertue described it as 'a fine dineing room (three noble portraits of 3 Speakers)', which included one of 'ye present Speaker Arthur Onslow'. In 1778 the same arrangement was recorded, and it is evident that the only other full-length portrait was of George I, which was probably hung over the chimneypiece. The other pictures were, as today, half-length family portraits.

FURNISHINGS IN 1778

They reflected the use of the room for dining. The side-tables were 'Two large marble Slabs on Mahogany Frames', and there were three 'mahogany oblong dining Tables', a 'Mahogany Dumb Waiter', two easy chairs ('Bergerre Chairs covered with Spanish Leather and Cushions') and 'Twelve mahogany Chairs, Leather Seats and brass nailed'. A barometer and 'eight day spring Clock' were the only other contents. At the windows were 'Four crimson morine Festoon Window Curtains with Cornices compleat', and there was a 'Wilton Carpet'.

DECORATION

To celebrate the creation of the Onslow earldom in 1801, the new Earl (who venerated his father Arthur, the Great Speaker) redecorated and refurnished the room. The dado, doors, doorcases and cornice were grained and gilded (previously they had been grey and white), and earl's coronets were placed prominently over the doors. Whereas in 1778, there was no chandelier, a heavy ormolu chandelier was hung, and the central ceiling rose and circular surround were gilded. The 1st Earl's scheme of 1801–14 survives, apart from the uncovering of the earlier paintwork of the cornice above the chimneypiece by Fowler *c.*1970, who also repainted the ceiling.

FURNITURE

The 1st Earl replaced the old furniture with the present pieces. *The massive mahogany side-tables* supported by eagles are in the style of William Kent. *The sideboard with Assyrian masks in the frieze* is reminiscent of the style of the collector and designer Thomas Hope (1769–1831). The rest of the furniture – the dining-table, wine-cooler, etc. – is also early 19th-century, apart from the dining-chairs of *c.*1760.

CHIMNEYPIECE

This was designed by Leoni in the 1720s, and is the plainest and most massive of his creations. The steel grate is early 19th-century and was presumably added by the 1st Earl. In 1778 there was a 'large steel Stove', reflecting the need for additional warmth in the north-west corner of the house.

WALLPAPER

The present wallpaper, very much in the style of the 1720s and '30s, is in fact an early 20th-century re-

The Speakers' Parlour

creation. Beneath, there are three layers, including two of the same 'Amberley' pattern – the first green, the second yellow (presumably made for the 4th Earl). Originally, the walls were hung with green distemper wallpaper.

MEMORABILIA

In recent years, the room has continued to develop as a shrine to the Onslow Speakers, and much of their memorabilia (particularly of Speaker Arthur Onslow) is displayed here.

PICTURE FRAMES

The elaborate picture frames were presumably added by the 1st Earl, given that they are in tune with the early 19th-century taste for bizarre eclecticism. The frames at either end of the room (surrounding the portraits of Speaker Arthur Onslow and his mentor, the 1st Lord Onslow) incorporate 17th-century carving with 18th- or early 19th-century additions (in particular the outer mouldings). The pair of eagles above the image of the Great Speaker is appropriate, as the eagle not only forms part of the Onslow crest, but is also an ancient symbol of power and victory, lavishly alluded to in the carving of the tables beneath. Eagles are also symbols of pride, which this room celebrates. The portrait of Sir Richard Onslow ('Speaker in the Reign of Queen Elizabeth') has a massive auricular frame, which could be 17th-century Italian, but is perhaps more likely to be an early 19th-century re-creation of such a grand frame.

PICTURES

FIREPLACE WALL, OVERDOOR, LEFT:

Attributed to HANS HYSING (1678–1752/3)
Lieutenant-General Richard Onslow (d.1760)
Younger brother of the Great Speaker, who, on inheriting the family estate, bought his brother a commission in the infantry. He rose to become, in 1741, Adjutant-General to the Forces. He was present at the victory of Dettingen in 1743, the last battle in which a British King (George II) personally commanded his troops. The distinctly archaic helmet on the table places this picture in the chivalric tradition of military portraiture.

OVERMANTEL:

THOMAS STEWARDSON (1781–1859)
George, 1st Earl of Onslow (1731–1814)
Son of the Great Speaker, and a prominent Whig politician. He was a favourite of George III, and is depicted here in the Windsor uniform that the King invented to distinguish the Royal Family and senior courtiers. His earl's robes are draped over the chair. Onslow was created Earl of Onslow in 1801, and may himself have placed this picture in the room that he embellished in celebration of the earldom (note the earl's coronets above the doorcase).

OVERDOOR, RIGHT:

ENGLISH, early 18th-century
Margaret, Lady Shelley (1696–1758)
Daughter of Thomas, 1st Lord Pelham, and sister of the Prime Minister, the 1st Duke of Newcastle, she was the wife of Sir John Shelley, 4th Bt of

The mahogany side-table supported by an eagle in the Speakers' Parlour is in the style of William Kent

Mickleham, Surrey. Their daughter, Henrietta, married the 1st Earl of Onslow in 1753.

EAST WALL (RIGHT OF FIREPLACE), OVERDOOR, LEFT:

Sir GODFREY KNELLER (1646/9–1723)
Elizabeth, Lady Onslow (1660/1–1718)
Daughter of Sir Henry Tulse, Lord Mayor of London, she married the 1st Lord Onslow in 1676. Painted – with the companion portrait of her husband, hanging opposite – *c.*1685, and of very high quality. Lady Onslow drowned herself the year after her husband's death. Both Kneller's portraits have been enlarged at the sides, presumably to fit the pair of frames *c.*1745.

OVERDOOR, CENTRE:

Attributed to HANS HYSING (1678–1752/3)
Arthur Onslow, the Great Speaker (1691–1768), Inscribed 1728
Son of Foote Onslow, he married, in 1720, Ann Bridges of Ember Court, Thames Ditton. Their son, George, inherited Clandon in 1776. Arthur was the most distinguished of the Onslow Speakers, holding the post from 1728 to 1761 and introducing various reforms, including the recording of parliamentary proceedings. He was also interested in the arts, forming a collection of portraits of famous Englishmen and becoming a Trustee of the British Museum. After his father's death in 1710, Arthur was taken up by his uncle, the 1st Lord Onslow, whose own distinguished tenure of the Speakership must have been an inspiring precedent (see his portrait as Speaker by Kneller hanging opposite).

There are numerous versions of the portrait (both full- and half-length), but this picture may be the original. According to the inscription, it was painted in 1728, the year of his election as Speaker.

OVERDOOR, RIGHT:

Sir GODFREY KNELLER (1646/9–1723)
Richard, 1st Lord Onslow (1654–1717)
Painted *c.*1685. For biography, see p. 57.

WEST WALL (OPPOSITE FIREPLACE):

ENGLISH, early 18th-century
Richard Onslow (1528–71)
Son of Roger Onslow and husband of Katherine Harding of Knoll, Surrey, he was a lawyer who was appointed Recorder of London (1563), and

The portrait of Richard Onslow, the Black Speaker, in the Speakers' Parlour is in a massive and ornate frame, which is either 17th-century Italian, or an early 19th-century revival of the same style

Chancellor of the Exchequer in 1714. There are conflicting accounts of his character, but he seems not to have been the 'trifling, vain man of ridiculous figure' (according to Lord Dartmouth), but rather Bishop Burnet's 'worthy man' who – in Queen Caroline's words – had 'something Great in his manner and carriage that drew a particular respect for him as soon as he was seen'. He was the revered 'Uncle Onslow' of Speaker Arthur Onslow, who became his secretary in 1714 and whose high opinion of him was shared by George I, who created him a peer in 1716. Like his successors in the peerage, and like Speaker Arthur Onslow, he was a Whig adherent of Sir Robert Walpole.

CLOCK

The longcase clock is the 'eight day Clock by Grigg [in fact signed Fra. Gregg] in a Walnut Tree Case' listed in the 'Stair Cases and Passages' in 1778.

MACE

On the sideboard opposite the fireplace is *an ebonised staff, carved to resemble bamboo with a silver finial*. This is probably a porter's staff. These were still used in great households in the late 17th and early 18th centuries, and were carried by the porter, who would greet all visitors, welcoming guests and driving away undesirables with foul language described by contemporaries as 'porterly'.

PORCELAIN

The early Worcester plates – some decorated with the Onslow coat of arms, others with a coronet – are early 19th-century.

The large tureens in the shape of fish are by the Italian designer G. P. V. Nove, *c.*1800.

Solicitor General (1566). He was elected Speaker in 1566 and held the post until his death. The inheritance of his wife's family estate at Knoll, near Cranleigh, established the Onslows in Surrey (previously they had lived in Shropshire). A 'very learned lawyer', he was known as the 'Black Speaker' on account of his swarthiness. Although this portrait is inscribed 1566, it is an early 18th-century pastiche, possibly painted for this room. Enoch Seeman (*c.*1694–1745) may have been the painter.

NORTH WALL (LEFT OF FIREPLACE):

Sir GODFREY KNELLER (1646/9–1723)
Richard, 1st Lord Onslow (1654–1717)
Painted in 1710, according to the inscription. MP for Guildford in 1678, he inherited Clandon as 2nd Baronet in 1688. He was elected Speaker in 1708, and continued in office until he was made

THE LIBRARY

The original use of this room is unclear, but it was certainly a library in 1778, and may well have been from the start. (There is, however, the possibility that it was originally the State Bedroom.) The focal point of the room in 1778 was – as it is again today – Thornhill and Hogarth's overmantel *View of the House of Commons* of 1730, with Speaker Arthur Onslow about to give the floor to his friend Sir Robert Walpole, the Prime Minister. This picture –

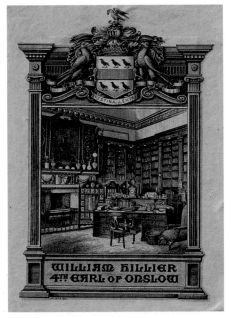

(Left) The 4th Earl's 1903 bookplate illustrates the Library (above) and has been used as the basis for the current arrangement

and Speaker Onslow's pictures and books – had come to Clandon on his son's inheritance of the Onslow title and estates in 1776. The future 1st Earl of Onslow installed the parliamentary picture in the Library overmantel, and also hung here the Speaker's collection of portraits of famous Englishmen. In acquiring these images, Speaker Onslow took some trouble to ensure their authenticity and their association with the sitters themselves. Thus his portrait of Milton had belonged to a relation of the poet and had been painted in his lifetime.

CONTENTS IN 1778

There were nineteen of Speaker Onslow's portraits here, including Shakespeare, Spenser and Dryden; Thomas Hobbes, the philosopher; several bishops;

27

and 'Sir Walter Raleigh' among others. Only one survived the 19th-century sales – a portrait of Chaucer. There were also two drawings and thirteen engravings (including portraits of Sidney, Virgil, Pope and Walpole), some ovals, in a mixture of gilt and 'ebony and gilt' frames. These pictures must have hung above and around a 'compleat Range of Library Book Cases', possibly the bookcases still in the room. Otherwise, the room contained library furniture: a 'mahogany Writing Table' and other tables; 'Ten Yew tree Elbow Chairs and Cushions'; 'a Globe and Frame'; an 'eight day spring Table Clock'; an 'Inkstand and silvered Furniture' and a 'Tea Caddy'. On the floor was a 'Tapestry pattern Carpet'.

In 1778 – as today – the overall colour of the upholstery was green: at the windows were 'Two green morine Festoon Window Curtains compleat', and one of the tables had a 'green Cover'. Sadly, most of these contents appear to have been dispersed subsequently, but the fixtures remain, including the 'oval Glass in an elegant carved Frame with ornaments' between the windows.

DECORATION

The 4th Earl's bookplate has been used as the basis for the arrangement of the furniture, including the writing-desk and fire-screen inset with numerous photographs of family and friends. The 4th Earl preserved the earlier 19th-century oak-grained scheme of decoration, but the room was completely redecorated in the late 1970s by Martin Drury with advice from Fowler, who also designed the textiles (the upholstery of the sofas) and carpet.

CHIMNEYPIECE

The marble chimneypiece is similar in style to those by Rysbrack in the Marble Hall, so must date from the 1720s. The superstructure seems to be later, and as the plaster medallions framing the overmantel painting are comparable to the plasterwork of the window reveals, they are presumably part of the 3rd Lord Onslow's alterations in the 1730s and '40s.

PLASTERWORK

The central section of the ceiling is thought to have been replaced following water damage. Only the rectangular band of plasterwork above the cove is in ornamental stucco of the 1720s. Elsewhere, in the window reveals and on the chimneypiece, the plasterwork looks more rococo and is therefore probably of the 1730s or '40s. It is comparable to the plasterwork of that date at Honington Hall, Warwickshire.

BOOKS

The Great Speaker's library was dispersed in 1885 but it clearly formed the core of the collection after 1776. It contained contemporary publications designed to be read for pleasure, as well as the inevitable legal and parliamentary works.

The 4th Earl managed to buy back some of the Speaker's books. The Speaker's armorial bookplate can still be found on some of the early books and is exceptional in having been designed by William Kent (his only *ex-libris*), and probably engraved by Benjamin Cole. The copper plate is in the Speakers' Parlour.

The library at Clandon was clearly designed to be used, by family and guests (and possibly by the household), and was not the exclusive preserve of an individual collector. The printed notice of 1819 still in the Library enjoins borrowers of books 'to *replace* them on the same shelf'.

Later generations of the family continued the tradition of utility and pleasure, adding numerous books on gardening, travel, sports and pastimes, as well as on politics, literature and history. Some are curious, and somewhat inexplicable, such as *Nudity in Modern Life* (1929) and *Among the Nudists* (1932), which carry the bookplate of the 4th Earl (though they must have belonged to the 5th Earl), as do numerous publications on New Zealand, where he was Governor in 1888–92.

FURNITURE

The marquetry and ebony writing-table (between the windows) is English, early 19th-century.

THE ONSLOW MUSEUM

Now a family museum, in 1778 this was Lord Onslow's dressing room adjacent to the State Bedroom. It is unclear where Lord Onslow slept, though it would presumably have been upstairs, as he would not have used the State Bedroom, which was the prerogative of particularly important guests.

A chairback upholstered with 'flamestitch' needlework to match the hangings on the State Bed

CONTENTS IN 1778

These included practical furniture, eg 'A mahogany Wardrobe and Chest of Drawers', 'A Glass in an oval carved Frame and ornaments', two tables and 'Six Bamboo Chairs and Cushions'. There was also a barometer and a 'small Wilton Carpet'. Otherwise it was arranged as a cabinet room for the display of pictures, sculpture and curiosities, some of which would have been kept in 'a small Cabinet'. Six of the eleven portraits were in 'oval Frames', and the sitters included historical characters (such as Queen Elizabeth I and the Earl of Leicester) as well as Lady Onslow and 'three other Family Portraits' (possibly pastels by Russell and Gardner). There were also 'Six small Bas-Reliefs', 'Thirteen Models and Medallions and one of Oliver Cromwell in Silver', a 'small half length' (presumably a portrait), 'a Head' and 'a Print'. The thickly hung walls were reflected in 'a concave mirror, a convex Ditto', and – presumably on the chimneypiece – were placed 'An Etruscan Urn and Four Figures'.

MUSEUM DISPLAY

The previous use of this room as a cabinet-cum-dressing room is consistent with its present arrangement as a family museum, with particular emphasis upon the 4th Earl's Governorship of New Zealand (1888–92). The most notable of the New Zealand objects presented to the 4th Earl is the Kiwi feather cloak. The ten-month-old Huia Onslow (the 4th Earl's youngest son) was wrapped in this cloak for his presentation to the Ngati Huia tribe. The cloak was, according with Maori ceremony, draped over his coffin.

THE STATE BEDROOM

Called the 'State Bedchamber' in 1778, this was presumably the original location of the Clandon State Bed, although the room may have begun life as a drawing room. In 1969–70, the State Bed was moved here from the Green Drawing Room (where it had been placed by the 4th Earl) to restore the 1778 status quo. At that time, Fowler also put up the red flock wallpaper, the design of which derives from a fragment found in the house. At the same time, the room was converted from a family museum.

CHIMNEYPIECE

The present painted wood chimneypiece (of the 1720s–'30s) was moved here from an upstairs bedroom in 1969–70, when the carved and pedimented chimneypiece and overmantel (of the 1730s–'40s) was moved upstairs.

PLASTERWORK

The ceiling and cornice are part of the original Leoni house and are presumably by Artari. The contrast between the rough and the smooth stucco – an effect previously more prominent in the Marble Hall – is particularly decorative. The half-naked goddess seated in the clouds is presumably Venus holding up the torch of love, a theme alluded to by the various cupids and putti, pairs of whom are holding up heavy swags of flowers and fruit in the cove. In the central roundel, Venus's torch frightens away the powers of darkness (symbolised by the fleeing winged creatures to the bottom right). One of the putti holds aloft a basket of roses (a flower sacred to Venus). The four medallions in the corners frame heads symbolising the four elements. The theme of love is entirely appropriate for a bedroom, as was the original green decoration (as green is the colour of Venus and of sleep) and may indicate that this was indeed the original function of the room.

STATE BED

As in 1778, the focus of the room is 'A noble costly Bedstead with Hangings beautifully worked in a great variety of Colours lined with Sattin and superbly finished'. This bed, its accompanying seat furniture and the 'Two pair of Satin Window Curtains with Cornices and Vallens [valances] fringed' (the pelmets are original) make up a suite of immensely costly textiles that was designed to impress by its extravagance. Made about 1710, probably by a royal craftsman for the old house at Clandon, they were not replaced partly because of the cost, but also no doubt as a symbol of the continuity and antiquity of the family. This also explains the presence here in 1778 of 'a curious wrought Purse in a glass Case' (now hanging to the right of the chimneypiece), Speaker Arthur Onslow's symbol of office as Chancellor of Queen Caroline of Ansbach, which was bequeathed to him on her

The State Bedroom

death in 1737. The bed has been reduced in height and converted to a four-poster at some stage in its history. Originally, the canopy would have been supported by a chain from the ceiling.

By family tradition, the last guest to sleep in the State Bed (in 1791) was the Princesse de Lamballe, a friend of Queen Marie-Antoinette, who suffered a gory fate at the hands of the Revolutionary mob. The bed was also used for lying-in-state: an ancient family retainer (the lodge keeper at Merrow) remembered paying his respects here to the corpse of the 1st Earl, who died in 1814. One might have thought that the Prince of Wales (the future George IV) would have used this room during his visits in the 1780s, but he was apparently lodged in the so-called 'Prince Regent's Bedroom' upstairs.

OTHER FURNISHINGS IN 1778

The other, rather sparse, furniture, was equally extravagant, including – between the windows – 'A large Pier Glass in a capital and elegantly carved gilt and burnished Frame', above a 'most beautiful Marble Slab on a superb carved gilt and burnished Frame'. As was often the case in State Bedrooms, there was a single, particularly grand, cabinet: 'A most curious and very beautiful Cabinet composed of Agate Egyptian Pebble Silver and Ebony and Rosewood with gilt ornaments etc.' Otherwise, the furniture was limited to 'A mahogany night Table' and 'A Pole Fire Screen', and the only carpet was 'A slip of Floor Cloth', presumably around three sides of the bed. (The baize fitted carpet and the mid-18th-century needlework rug – both installed in the *c.*1970 restoration – give an erroneous impression of a richly carpeted room.) The nine pictures comprised six portraits (including five of

the Pelham family in 'rich carved and gilt Frames'
– three of which are now in the Saloon) and three
landscapes.

PICTURES

SOUTH WALL, OPPOSITE FIREPLACE, LEFT,
ABOVE:

After SIR ANTHONY VAN DYCK? (1599–1641)
John, 1st Lord Finch of Fordwich (1584–1660)
Speaker of the House of Commons and Lord
Keeper, Finch was also influential in court circles,
being on familiar terms with Queen Henrietta
Maria and the Queen of Bohemia. He acted as a
mediator between King and Parliament, and in
1633, on behalf of the Inns of Court, organised a
masque in honour of Charles I. His loyalty to the
crown led to his impeachment, the sequestration of
his estates and exile in Holland. In 1660 he had the
satisfaction of being appointed to try the regicides,
but died before the proceedings began. This is a
copy of a lost portrait, generally, but perhaps
wrongly, attributed to Van Dyck.

BELOW, LEFT:

Manner of Sir GODFREY KNELLER (1646/9–1723)
Foote Onslow (1655–1710)
Son of Sir Arthur Onslow, 2nd Bt, by his second
wife, Mary Foote, daughter of Sir Thomas Foote,
1st Bt, Lord Mayor of London. This explains the
unusual Christian name. He married in 1687
Susannah Anlaby of Elton, near Hull, and their
two sons were Arthur Onslow, the Great Speaker,
and Lieutenant-General Richard Onslow. Foote
Onslow (MP for Guildford, 1688) lived beyond his
means, according to his son, the Speaker, and 'had
also very sore losses in his business and a very
numerous house to maintain, and not being the best
manager of his affairs neither, … that it very much
hastened his end'. None the less, he was 'a man of
true worth, and very solicitous for the good of his
family, tender to the greatest degree of me, and ever
anxious about my education …'.

SOUTH WALL, CENTRE, ABOVE:

Manner of Sir GODFREY KNELLER (1646/9–1723)
Susannah Anlaby (d. 1715)
Wife of Foote Onslow (m. 1687); of an old Yorkshire family, she found it difficult to come to terms
with her own family's reduced circumstances after

her extravagant husband's death in 1710. Her son,
Speaker Arthur Onslow, described her as 'an excellent woman in most respects' and 'although she had
rather too quick a spirit, she was a very good and in
most things a very wise woman: and she had in her
younger years been extremely handsome'.

BELOW:

JOHN RUSSELL, RA (1745–1806)
Traditionally called *Henrietta, Countess of Onslow*
(1730/1–1802)
Signed and dated 1769
This cannot be the 1st Earl's wife, as she was only 38
in 1769, and the sitter is a much older woman. This
is one of Russell's infrequent portraits in oils.

RIGHT, ABOVE:

ENGLISH, 17th-century
John Anlaby
Grandfather of Susannah Anlaby, the mother of
the Great Speaker. A prominent Puritan, he was
present when Charles I's death warrant was signed,
but, according to Speaker Onslow, 'his name is not
to the warrant, which induces me to hope and
believe he approved not of it'.

BELOW:

ENGLISH, 17th-century
Sir Arthur Onslow, 2nd Bt (1622–88)
Son of Sir Richard Onslow, who purchased
Clandon in 1641. Both Sir Arthur's wives – Rose
Stoughton and Mary Foote – were heiresses. His
eldest son was created 1st Lord Onslow in 1716,
while his second son – Foote Onslow – was father
of the Great Speaker and grandfather of the 1st Earl
of Onslow.

FIREPLACE (NORTH) WALL, LEFT OF
CHIMNEYPIECE:

? ANGLO-DUTCH, 17th- or 18th-century
A Lake Scene
Possibly a fragment of a larger picture, in a vaguely
Claudean style, but the figures have a Dutch
derivation and the treatment of the foliage is
reminiscent of the Roman painter Andrea Locatelli
(1660–1741).

OVERMANTEL:

ENGLISH, early 18th-century
Richard, 1st Lord Onslow (1654–1717)
This penetrating image of Lord Onslow in old age

may be by the Swedish painter Hans Hysing, to whom several other portraits at Clandon are attributed. Lord Onslow was the mentor of his nephew, Arthur Onslow, the Great Speaker, who described him as 'a person of great probity, courage and honour'. It was in 1710, around the time of this portrait, that the nineteen-year-old Arthur Onslow's father died. Lord Onslow then treated him 'as his second son, received me in his house as if I had been so, and endeavoured to make the world look upon me as such'. On Lord Onslow's appointment as Chancellor of the Exchequer in 1714, he saved the young Arthur's finances by appointing him as secretary, by securing another sinecure and 'by the help of these incomes I preserved myself and my family too'. This was prescient, as Arthur Onslow's son was to inherit Clandon and become the 1st Earl of Onslow.

FURNITURE

Apart from the State Bed and its suite of upholstered furniture, the rest of the contents were acquired by Mrs Gubbay. They include *Anglo-Dutch marquetry tables* of 1680–90, *lacquer mirrors* of *c.*1700, *a pair of engraved glass sconces* of *c.*1690 (on either side of the State Bed), *a green and gold lacquer small secretaire cum dressing-cabinet* of *c.*1710 and a remarkable *satinwood writing- and dressing-table and mirror*, inlaid with chinoiserie marquetry and with

The chinoiserie marquetry writing- and dressing-table in the State Bedroom may have been made in Thomas Chippendale's workshop

pagoda crestings (opposite the fireplace), which is very similar to designs in Chippendale's *Director*, and may have come from his workshop. It was originally at Longford Castle, Wiltshire.

THE STONE STAIRCASE

This is a staircase on a grand scale, but its decoration is extremely subdued. The iron balustrade, for example, could not be more plain (it was originally painted bronze and green). The original colour scheme reflected the present name – ie it was painted stone throughout – but when the Speakers' Parlour was redecorated between 1801 and 1814, the doorcases, doors and dado were grained to match.

This staircase connects the basement with all the main floors of the house. This made it an important thoroughfare, both for family and staff. One of the principal links was between the Speakers' Parlour (always a dining room) and the kitchen directly beneath. There is also a possibility that there was originally another large dining room on the first floor, but the great distance would have made this rather impractical and also one would have expected a much grander and more ceremonial approach than is provided by this spacious but plain staircase hall. The Oak Staircase is therefore unlikely to have acted as a formal link between rooms of state at ground- and first-floor levels. There is no record of any curtains or blinds in 1778, but by 1899 there were 'crimson figured silk damask window curtains' and red blinds.

PICTURES

FOOT OF STAIRS:

The group of horse paintings, at the foot of the stairs and on the lower landing, is by John Ferneley (1782–1860), who was commissioned to paint the stud at Melton Mowbray of the 3rd Lord Gardner, whose daughter Florence married the 4th Earl of Onslow in 1875 and thereby brought the pictures to Clandon. Ferneley's emphasis is very much on the horses, and the landscape settings are perfunctory. The portraits range in date between 1830 and 1850, and represent hunters rather than racehorses. Melton Mowbray is still famous as the centre of the greatest hunting country in England.

Southern-Mouthed Hounds; by Francis Barlow (Stone Staircase)

FURNITURE

The massive giltwood armchair, c.1720–30, is akin to the throne chairs made for the London livery companies and for London clubs. The head of such bodies would presumably have used them as symbols of office, and much as royal throne-chairs were used by the monarch. The original purpose of the Clandon chair is unknown, but may be associated with royal visits to Clandon or with the 2nd Lord Onslow's chairmanship (1720–3) of the Royal Exchange Assurance Corporation. Alternatively, it may have been made for the crown, and be a perk, perhaps relating to the speakership.

TOP OF STAIRS:

JOHN WOOTTON (1678/82–1764)
Horse and Jockey
This huge portrait of a grey held by a jockey in the Onslow pink racing colours was painted in 1715, and its scale and conception anticipate such equestrian portraits as Stubbs's *Hambletonian*, exhibited 1800 (National Trust, Mount Stewart). The setting is probably the nearby racecourse at Merrow Down, where the Whitsun meetings – under the auspices of the Onslows – were famous.

FRANCIS BARLOW (*c.*1626–1704)
A Farmyard
Already in 1656 John Evelyn described Barlow as 'the famous Paynter of fowle Beastes & Birds'. This is one of three vast canvases (100 × 136 inches; one is dated 1667, see p. 36) painted for Sir Robert Parkhurst at Pyrford Court, Surrey, and bought by Denzil Onslow in 1677. Onslow died in 1721, when he must have bequeathed the pictures to his great-nephew, the 2nd Lord Onslow, who rebuilt

Clandon in the 1720s. They were certainly hanging in the Saloon in 1778, and were presumably hung there from the beginning. In all, there are seven paintings by Barlow at Clandon, the largest collection of his work in a country house.

FRANCIS BARLOW (*c.*1626–1704)
Southern-Mouthed Hounds
Such hounds were 'thick-skinned and slow-footed … most proper for such as delight to follow them on foot', according to Richard Blome's *The Gentleman's Recreation* (1686). Probably part of the group of pictures by Barlow from Pyrford Court.

THE BLUE CHINA ROOM

A bedroom in 1778, and the 'Yellow Bedroom' in 1899, it was converted into a display room for porcelain in the early 1970s, when the Gubbay collection (see p. 89) was installed at Clandon and it was christened the Blue China Room.

FURNISHINGS IN 1778

The curtains were yellow damask festoons, *en suite* with an adjoining dressing room. The 'Four post Bedstead' was covered with chintz, although the gilt seat furniture was upholstered in green silk damask. The remainder of the useful furniture was either mahogany or japanned.

PICTURES

WEST (ENTRANCE) WALL, ABOVE DOOR:

JOHN RUSSELL, RA (1745–1806)
Rural Employment
Signed and dated 1786
Depicts the artist's daughters feeding chickens. Russell was a friend of the 1st Earl of Onslow,

so it is particularly appropriate that this picture (and the dummy board of the same subject, shown by the fireplace) should have been loaned to Clandon. They were painted for Stubbers in Essex, and are loaned by a descendant of the first owner.

WEST (ENTRANCE) WALL, LEFT OF DOOR:

REX WHISTLER (1905–44)
Hannah Gubbay (c.1886–1968)
Daughter of E.D. Ezra and Mozelle Sassoon, and wife of David Gubbay (opposite). Mr and Mrs Gubbay were first cousins, and were therefore both cousins of the flamboyant collector Sir Philip Sassoon, with whom Mrs Gubbay collaborated on an important series of annual London exhibitions beginning in 1929. Wealthy in her own right, she also inherited money and property from Sir Philip. In 1968 she bequeathed her various collections to the National Trust, and Clandon was restored for their display. Whistler was a fashionable painter of *trompe-l'oeil* decorations (eg at Plas Newydd and Mottisfont) and occasionally painted portraits on a small scale.

RIGHT OF DOOR:

JOHN SINGER SARGENT (1856–1925)
David Gubbay (d. 1929)
Husband of Mrs Gubbay, he was a financier who managed the considerable commercial and private affairs of Sir Philip Sassoon. The commission may

A Chelsea sunflower dish and melon tureen, c.1755, from the Gubbay collection

have derived from Sargent's employment by Sir Philip Sassoon and his sister, Sybil, Marchioness of Cholmondeley.

FURNITURE

The early 19th-century ebony inlaid mahogany display cases were probably made for Clandon. *The other display cases*, originally purchased for Mrs Gubbay's house, Little Trent Park, are of high quality in their own right, especially those on either side of the entrance door: one in Chinese Chippendale style, the other a black-japanned break-front cabinet of c.1800.

The overmantel glass – the arched centre decorated with armorials in *verre églomisé* – was made for Hill Hall, Essex. The arms are of Smith impaling Hedges, for Sir Edward Smith, Bt, of Hill Hall, who married Ann Hedges. Sir Edward inherited in 1714, remodelled the house and placed an identical coat of arms on the pediment of the new east front, which is dated 1714. His wife died in 1719, so the mirror (stylistically c.1715) fits neatly into the history of the house. Mrs Gubbay placed it – rather incongruously – behind her bed at Little Trent Park, so that it acted as a quasi-headboard.

CERAMICS, ENAMELS, JADE, CRYSTAL, METALWORK AND GLASS

Here is shown the bulk of Mrs Gubbay's collection of English and continental porcelain and earthenware. All the principal factories are represented with the emphasis on Bow, Chelsea, Derby and

Tournai ice pail from the service ordered by the Duc d'Orléans in 1787 (Gubbay collection, Blue China Room)

Staffordshire, as well as Meissen and Sèvres. In addition to the most sophisticated porcelain, Mrs Gubbay also had a penchant for the more vernacular productions of the English pottery manufacturers. Her collection is also strong in Chinese porcelain and decorative works of art in various media.

THE STATE DINING ROOM

Since about 1970, this room has been known as the State Dining Room on the assumption that it was where Frederick, Prince of Wales was entertained to a grand pre-racing luncheon in 1729. However, there is no evidence for this, apart from the fact that the royal entertainment took place 'above stairs'. In fact, the Prince's 1729 meal was probably taken on the principal floor (see p. 66). One of the reasons for this is the apparently unfinished decoration of this room (plain walls and ceiling), and the fact that the chimneypieces are of a type at Clandon that appears to have been added by the 3rd Lord Onslow in the 1730s or '40s, when he finished off the Leoni house commissioned by his father. It was called the 'East Rooms' in 1899, because the space was partitioned by the 4th Earl in the 1880s to provide an extra dressing room. The room was extensively restored and painted yellow in the early 1970s.

FURNISHINGS IN 1778

The room was provided with 'an exceeding good full sized Billiard Table '… with Maces Cues and Balls compleat', and was very richly furnished and hung thickly with pictures. The pier-glasses were 'carved and gilt' with 'a pair large marble Slabs on carved Frames' beneath. The seat furniture was walnut and mahogany, and there were two 'six leaved Japan screens'. Also listed was much 'ornamental China', five busts, no fewer than 38 portraits (including several of famous Englishmen, presumably from the Great Speaker's collection) and seven other pictures. As well as being something of a gallery, the room served as a repository for 'Two Port Folios and Seventy Prints'.

PICTURES

SOUTH WALL, OVERMANTEL:

Attributed to HANS HYSING (1678–1752/3)
Lieutenant-General Richard Onslow (d. 1760)
For biography, see p. 25. This portrait is related to another attributed to Hysing in the Speakers' Parlour and is inscribed 174? on the turned-over edge of the canvas.

RIGHT OF CHIMNEYPIECE:

Attributed to FRANCIS BARLOW (c.1626–1704)
A Gardener
Generally attributed to Barlow, and therefore associated with the group of pictures from Pyrford Court, but possibly by Leonard Knyff, who painted a bird's-eye view of Clandon in 1708 and was influenced by Barlow. The initials 'R.O.' on the cupboard may be an allusion to Richard Onslow – presumably either Sir Richard (1601–64) or his grandson, the 1st Lord Onslow (1654–1717). Judging by the tools, and the glimpse of garden, the sitter is likely to have been a gardener.

WEST WALL (FACING WINDOWS), LEFT OF DOOR:

FRANCIS BARLOW (c.1626–1704)
Landscape with Birds and Fishes
Signed and dated 1667
One of three large canvases painted by Barlow for Pyrford Court in the 1660s (this is the only one to be dated).

RIGHT OF DOOR:

FRANCIS BARLOW (c.1626–1704)
A Decoy
Defoe described Pyrford as 'exceeding pleasant, especially for the most Beautiful intermixture of Wood, and Water in the Park, and Gardens, and Grounds adjoining … particularly in one thing which is not found in all that part of England; namely a Duckoy, which adjoins to his Park, and which makes the rest inimitably agreeable.'

NORTH (FIREPLACE WALL), OVERMANTEL:

Attributed to JOHN MICHAEL WRIGHT (?1617–94)
Sir Richard Onslow, Bt (1601–64)
Known as the 'Red Fox of Surrey' for his equivocal attachment to the Parliamentary cause in the Civil War, Sir Richard was created baronet in 1624 and bought Clandon in 1641 from the Weston family.

The State Dining Room

A Decoy; by Francis Barlow, 1667 (State Dining Room)

FURNITURE

The Gubbay pieces include *the two pier-glasses*, probably the most important of all Mrs Gubbay's numerous mirrors, not only retaining their bevelled Vauxhall plates, but also their *verre églomisé* frames incorporating on a red and black ground gilt designs after Jean Bérain (1637–1711), *maître-ornemaniste* to Louis XIV and the master of Daniel Marot. A very similar pier-glass made for William III *c.*1695 is at Hampton Court. Several *early 18th-century chairs, sofas and a tripod-table* (mainly *c.*1730) are upholstered with important needlework in remarkable condition, including a walnut sofa covered in velvety silk *petit point*, which enhances the bloom of the peaches and other fruits incorporated into the design; *the mahogany tripod tea-table inlaid with mother-of-pearl and brass* (at the north end of the room to the left of the chimneypiece) is attributed to the German cabinetmaker Frederick Hintz, who advertised the sale of such inlaid furniture in London in 1738.

The *library table* was commissioned from Chippendale by Sir Lawrence Dundas in 1764 for Moor Park, Hertfordshire. In the early 20th century it was acquired by the leading furniture dealers Partridges and sold to Sir Henry Price of Wakehurst Place. In 1963, Sir Henry bequeathed Wakehurst Place, with a generous endowment, to the National Trust. In 2005 it was moved to Clandon for its better conservation and display.

The comparatively few Onslow pieces displayed here include *a huge painted leather screen* of *c.*1700.

TEXTILE PICTURES

On the window wall are portraits in *petit point* of *Queen Caroline of Ansbach* (1683–1737), consort of George II, and of the King himself. These acquisitions by Mrs Gubbay are particularly appropriate at Clandon, given Speaker Onslow's service to the Queen as her Chancellor.

Above the central door opposite the windows is a

particularly rare knotted panel – made in the same way as a carpet – depicting a kingfisher, a male golden pheasant and a male wood duck disporting themselves at Claremont, Esher, the famous garden of the Prime Minister, the 1st Duke of Newcastle. The grotto and the island temple still survive – as do the gardens – in the care of the National Trust. The panel is signed 'Parisot' for Peter Parisot (1697–after 1766), whose manufactory at Fulham employed *emigrés* from the Savonnerie textile factory. The Duke of Newcastle invested in the enterprise in 1754, but despite the high quality of its productions, Parisot was forced to sell up in 1755. Gubbay collection.

PORCELAIN

Flanking the chimneypieces are *three pairs of Chinese porcelain cranes* (1723–35) and *one pair of ducks* on mid-18th-century giltwood brackets. Gubbay collection.

THE GREEN DAMASK BEDROOM
(THE 'PRINCE REGENT'S BEDROOM')

From about 1970 it was called the Prince Regent's Bedroom, but there is no historical evidence for this name, so the 1899 inventory description has been substituted.

FURNISHINGS IN 1778

The windows were hung with 'Two sets of green silk Damask Festoon Window Curtains', matching the upholstery of the six 'mahogany French Elbow chairs', so green certainly persisted as the predominant colour of the textiles. However, in 1778 the four-poster bed 'of wainscot with mahogany Feet Pillars' was hung with chintz. As in the Yellow Bedroom, there was only one portrait (of 'King Charles') which was presumably hung over the 'sconce Glass in a carved and gilt Pediment Frame' above the chimneypiece. Between the windows was a giltwood pier-table with a 'large and beautiful variegated Marble Slab'. There was much porcelain: 'Sixteen pieces fine Antique ornamental China'.

WALLPAPER

The red flock paper of 'Amberley' pattern dates from the 1720s or early 1730s, and is therefore contemporary with the building of the house. The survival of the original paper fillet around the borders of the paper (in Greek-key pattern) is particularly rare. This paper was rediscovered about 1970, and was found to be in remarkably good state (as in the Green Drawing Room below). The two colours – crimson and cream – simulate in wallpaper the effect of a two-colour damask. The crimson perhaps signified that this room was used by important guests.

PICTURES

OVERDOORS:

The pair of fancy portraits of a boy and girl are copies after the Swiss painter ALEXIS GRIMOU (c.1680–1740), and the portrait of the 1st Earl of Onslow by THOMAS STEWARDSON (1781–1859) is derived from the full-length in the Speakers' Parlour (see p. 25).

OVERMANTEL:

PHILIP DE LASZLO (1869–1937)
Richard, 5th Earl of Onslow (1876–1945)
Diplomat, politician, antiquarian and the historian of the Onslow family. His wife was also painted by de Laszlo (in 1929, see p. 21).

WINDOW WALL, LEFT:

ALAN SUTHERLAND
William, 6th Earl of Onslow (1913–71)
Soldier, awarded the Military Cross in the Western Desert, 1942; father of the present Earl. Commissioned in 1984 by his second wife, Jo, Countess of Onslow.

CENTRE:

Attributed to GERRIT (GERARD) VAN HONTHORST (1590–1656)
St Jerome
This picture is clearly influenced by Caravaggio, and Honthorst is one of several northern painters who assimilated his style in Rome. Born in Utrecht, the pupil of Abraham Bloemaert, Honthorst returned to Holland in the 1620s, and was invited to England by Charles I. This picture from the Woodbine Parish family collection was

St Jerome; attributed to Gerrit van Honthorst (Green Damask Bedroom)

acquired by the 1st Lord Rendel for nearby Hatchlands Park.

RIGHT OF CHIMNEYPIECE, ABOVE:

ENGLISH SCHOOL, 19th century
Lt General William Francis Bentinck Loftus
The general's daughter, Mary, married in 1848, George Onslow, nephew of the 3rd Earl of Onslow. Their son, William Hillier Onslow, inherited Clandon in 1870, when he became 4th Earl.

BELOW:

ENGLISH SCHOOL, c.1860
Portrait of an officer in old age
He is wearing Crimean and Indian Mutiny medals.

OPPOSITE WINDOWS, LEFT:

THOMAS BEACH (1738–1806)
Charles Penruddock
Beach was a Dorset painter who trained under Sir Joshua Reynolds and was based in London and Bath, from where he travelled in Dorset and

Somerset painting portraits of the local gentry. This and the following portrait are on loan from the executors of Col N. E. Penruddock.

RIGHT:

THOMAS BEACH (1738–1806)
John Hungerford Penruddock

OPPOSITE CHIMNEYPIECE:

LEENDERT (LEONARD) KNYFF (1650–1722)
Clandon Park
Signed and dated 1708
This panoramic view depicts the old house at Clandon built by the Weston family around 1600, which was demolished in the 1720s to make way for Leoni's new house. The main drive from Merrow is shown in the foreground, while the house is surrounded by formal gardens. The stable block to the left of the main house was preserved by Leoni, and was not demolished until the stables were rebuilt near Temple Court by 'Capability' Brown in the 1780s.

FURNITURE

ON PIER:

The scagliola-topped oak table is Italian, c.1650. The coat of arms has not been identified. This is an Onslow piece, but its provenance is unknown, which is unfortunate, as it is a great rarity in an English country house.

The massive bureau-plât or writing-table in the Louis XV style is French, c.1870.

FLANKING CHIMNEYPIECE:

A small chinoiserie cabinet c.1750, incorporating decorative japanned panels and a cresting in the form of a pagoda.

OVERMANTEL:

Overmantel glass, English, c.1690, acquired by Mrs Gubbay from Lord North's collection. The Vauxhall mirror plate is engraved and the frame is decorated in *verre églomisé* with strapwork, flowers and husks.

The remaining furniture from the Gubbay collection includes *a pair of settees* in a hybrid Gothick/Chinese style, upholstered in *petit point*, c.1765, and a *breakfast-table* decorated with Chinese fretwork, c.1750.

THE MARBLE HALL GALLERY

The open gallery overlooking the Marble Hall acts as a link between the two main staircases, as well as providing access to the three first-floor rooms in the centre of the east front.

It has been arranged to display porcelain, mainly from the Gubbay and Forde collections. The colour scheme is John Fowler's *c.*1970; presumably, it would have originally matched the paintwork of the Marble Hall.

FURNISHINGS IN 1778

It was very simply furnished with 'Two Scotch Carpets twenty three Yards', three 'Bell Lamps brass Frames Burners Glass Shades and Chains' and a wall lamp equivalent. There was an 'eight day clock wainscot case by Stedman' and, most interestingly, 'The Model of a Mansion, a Cabinet and Frame', perhaps of Clandon itself.

PORCELAIN

Here is displayed part of Mrs Gubbay's collection of continental porcelain figurines, and in two separate cabinets, the exceptional collection of Meissen *commedia dell'arte* figures compiled by Ivo Forde, which is loaned to the National Trust by his family. Mr Forde's interest was sparked in 1952 by the purchase of a Derby figure, and other English models followed. Soon, however, he fell under the spell of Meissen, determining to concentrate on the productions of the famous modeller J.J. Kaendler, whose 'early Baroque figures modelled at Meissen between 1738 and 1745 stood out in quality from anything I had yet seen'. Between 1959 and 1968 'I was lucky to find eight of the ten early great Harlequins of Kaendler, seven of his Italian Comedy Groups of the same period, together with a number of smaller Comedy figures by Kaendler and others from the set made by Peter Reinicke for the Duke of Weissenfels'. He also bought similar figures by other factories, mainly Italian Comedy characters which came from dealers in England, America, France and Belgium. With quality as the paramount criterion, Mr Forde declared that 'collecting these figures has been an unending source of pleasure to me'. The loan of 21 Meissen figures by Kaendler to Clandon – where Mrs Gubbay's outstanding collection was already on show – has ensured that the house is a veritable place of pilgrimage for the study of such porcelain figures and groups.

The Marble Hall Gallery also contains Mrs Gubbay's collection of framed early 19th-century Derby and Vienna floral plaques; and an exceptionally rare *Canton portrait figure (1730–40) of Henry Talbot of Churt Park, Dorking*, on loan from

The Meissen monkey orchestra created by J.J. Kaendler (Marble Hall Gallery)

the Dorking Museum. Only fifteen such figures survive. Talbot was an East India Company merchant, and Canton was the principal port for trade with China.

FURNITURE

The brass-bound leather chest engraved with the royal arms and with the hinges headed by a crown is English, c.1700. It probably belonged to Richard, 1st Lord Onslow, who was Chancellor of the Exchequer (1714-15), a post with which these trunks are traditionally associated.

THE STAIRS TO THE BASEMENT

PICTURES

The set of four engravings depicting hare hunting is by Bernard Baron, 1726, after lost paintings by John Wootton, commissioned by Edward Harley, 2nd Earl of Oxford. The engravings are extremely rare, probably because the pirated versions extinguished the demand for the expensive originals (Wootton paid Baron £50 for each plate and £3 for each print). The prints served as the source for the tapestries in the Hunting Room upstairs, which suggests that the 2nd Lord Onslow – the builder of Clandon, and the Master of a pack of harriers – may have played an important role in the financing of this series.

THE BASEMENT

The basement has been much altered and now contains utilities – shop, restaurant, kitchens, lavatories – and the Queen's Royal Surrey Regiment Museum so that it is difficult to establish the original uses of the rooms. The main entrance was always at the north, and a central corridor bisected the basement as at Coleshill, Berkshire, Beningbrough, Yorkshire, and the contemporary Houghton Hall, Norfolk. As at Houghton, the basement may have included family rooms – for informal dining and business – as well as the usual kitchen and service rooms. Today, however, only the Kitchen and its adjoining Pastry Room survive largely untouched, and both rooms were completely renovated during the 4th Earl's restoration in the 1870s. The location of the Servants' Hall, for example, is not known, despite the survival of its famous 18th-century rules board (shown in the passage outside the kitchen), and what was probably its table c.1730. This is the pine table with Tuscan-column legs now in the Restaurant.

THE KITCHEN

The Kitchen appears to have been completely refitted between 1870 and 1874. Virtually nothing survives from the earlier period, except for the butcher's block, which had been moved in here from a wet larder or meat room, probably after the property came to the National Trust in 1956.

The fireplace is of considerable interest. It is an Oxford Roasting Range supplied by Benham & Sons of Wigmore Street, London. This model was first installed in the early 1840s in the kitchens of the Reform Club, when they were being refitted by Alexis Soyer, who was later to distinguish himself by organising the supply and preparation of food to the army in the Crimea.

The spoon rack on the left of the fireplace was probably another Benham item, being illustrated on p. 621 of Soyer's *Regenerator*.

Further to the left, a Benham's *steam (or hot-water) heated hot-closet* incorporates a hotplate top for the serving hatch. From here, the food was carried by footmen up the stairs to the Speakers' Parlour.

Left again, a large niche is fitted with a sheet-iron smoke/steam hood. In this area a Benham's stove, probably incorporating one or more ovens, and hotplates, must have been fitted in the early 1870s, a Benham's soot-door still remaining in the back wall. After some twenty years of use, this was replaced with the present range, which incorporates two large ovens, a hotplate and a firebox fitted with Eagle-type falling firebars. The Eagle Range, the most popular cooking range in late Victorian England, was patented around the mid-1870s.

RULES to be Observed in this HALL.

1 WHOEVER is last at Breakfast to clear the Table, and put the Copper, Horns, Salt, Pepper &c, in their proper places, *or forfeit* _____ — 3

2 THE servants hall Cloth laid for Dinner by 1 o'Clock, and not omit laying the Salt, Pepper, and Spoons. _____ — 3

3 THE Housekeepers room Knives to be Clean'd evry day by the Usher of this hall. _____ — 3

4 THAT if any Person be heard to Swear, or Use any Indecent language at any time when the Cloth is on the table, *He is to forfeit.* _____ — 3

5 WHOEVER leaves any thing belonging to their Dress or any Wearing Apparel out of their proper places. — 3

6 THAT no one be suffered to Play at Cards in the Hall, before six o'Clock in the Evening. _____ — 3

7 WHOEVER leaves any Pieces of Bread at Breakfast, Dinner, or Supper. _____ — 1

8 THAT if any one shall be observ'd cleaning livery clothes, or leather breeches, at any time of Meals, or shall leave any dirt after cleaning them at any time. — 3

9 THAT the Usher to have the Hall decently Swept, and the dirt taken away before dinner time. _____ — 3

10 THAT no one shall put any kind of provisions in any Cupboard or Drawer in the Hall after their meals, but shall return it from whence they had it. _____ — 3

11 THAT the Table Cloth shall after all meals be folded up, and put in the drawer for that purpose. _____ — 3

12 THAT if any one be observ'd wipeing their Knives in the table cloth at any time. _____ — 3

13 THAT if any stable or other servant take any plates to the stable, or be seen to set them for Dogs to eat off _____ — 3

14 THAT no wearing apparel to hang in the Hall, but shall be put in the Closets for that Purpose. _____ — 3

15 ALL stable and other servants to come to dinner with their Coats on. _____ — 3

The 18th-century rules board (Basement corridor)

THE GARDEN

The impressive formal garden at Clandon, as shown in Knyff's painting of 1708, was probably laid out during the ownership of Sir Richard Onslow (1654–1717), later 1st Baron Onslow. Friend and neighbour of the diarist and gardener John Evelyn, Lord Onslow followed gardening fashions introduced to England by William and Mary after their accession in 1689. Clandon was one of only a handful of gardens of this size and splendour in England, on a par with those at Chatsworth, Badminton and Wilton. Formal gardens, which required manicured lawns, crisp topiary and regular bedding out of seasonal flowers, demanded intensive labour to maintain them. It is not known who laid out the garden at Clandon nor who tended it. (It is tempting to link Thomas Knight, a gardener listed in the Clandon Parish Register for 1709, with the Onslows, but this may be wishful thinking.)

In common with other gardens of the period, the most formal areas were close to the house, in order both to reflect the formality of the architecture in the planting, and to give a pleasant view from the windows. By the east front were a pair of large grass plats ornamented with standard shrubs in white painted tubs (perhaps bay or orange trees) and topiary shrubs (probably yew or holly). On the south side, to either side of the Bowling Green, were flower-beds bordered by low hedges and a pool at their centre. A more elaborate parterre lay further east, with narrow beds of florists' flowers (probably including tulips, marigolds and stock). These three areas were bordered by clipped yew hedges. Overlooking these highly decorative beds, or *plates-bandes*, was a terrace with a pool and fountain, rather like that at the Privy Garden at Hampton Court Palace (the best living guide to the style). Terraces and raised walks were popular, because they allowed a view over the complex designs of the parterres and spectators to watch those playing

at bowls below. Beyond the parterres and pools were avenues and an eye-catching mount. The mount, with its spiral walk to the summit, was intended as a viewpoint from which to see the house and the designs of the gardens below.

The kitchen garden lay within the pleasure ground, to the east of the house on the edge of the formal garden. To the west of the house was a wooded wilderness garden with serpentine paths ending in small grassed clearings with covered seats or sculpture at their centres. In 1729 Frederick, Prince of Wales lunched at Clandon and afterwards took a turn in the garden. Sir John Evelyn wrote that the Prince 'walkt round part of the garden and into the orangery in the midst of a wilderness of greens...'. The orangery at the centre of the wilderness garden was a circular or oval arena, lined with concentric rows of orange trees in tubs, interspersed with gravel walks. At its centre was a single tree, with a circular seat at its base. The orange trees would have been set out in the garden for the summer months and brought inside during the winter in order to protect them from frost. Unusually, there appears not to have been an orangery or similar conservatory building in or near this garden, so the orange trees would have needed to be transported some distance to the shelter of the house each autumn. In addition to the formal pools with fountains, there was a canal to the north of the house. This was probably an existing pond or lake which was enlarged and formalised. It was enclosed within a yew hedge, and the canal edge was laid to lawn and planted with topiary and an avenue of trees. The entire pleasure ground was surrounded by avenues and groves of trees and parkland grazed by deer.

The next phase in the garden at Clandon is shown in a plan, 'Severall Grounds Belonging to the Parish of Clandon', dating from the 1720s,

Knyff's 1708 bird's-eye view probably shows the formal garden laid out by the 1st Lord Onslow

when the new house was planned or under construction. This shows that the formal gardens had been simplified in their design since 1708. The parterres were replaced by the 'Gravell Garden' with lawns punctuated by topiary and the forecourt to the house was transformed into a 'Sweep open Terras for coaches'. The kitchen garden was now off the map – banished to the nearby home farm of Temple Court. The grass mount survived the changes and was described as 'a design'd Belvidere'. The domestic offices (uncomfortably close to the house) were reduced in size, and 'A very Large Fine Lawn' took their place. The demolition of these buildings and the enlarged lawn would have given improved views both to and from the new house.

The gardens underwent change once again in the 1740s, under the discerning eye of Richard, 3rd Baron Onslow, who was also finishing the interior of the house begun by his father. As with the house, the garden was made more fashionable and in keeping with Leoni's Palladian house. A more naturalistic style of gardening, as practised by the artist and landscape gardener William Kent, was popular amongst many of the Onslows' Whig friends and neighbours. Kent advised at Claremont, the Duke of Newcastle's garden, and at Esher Place, that of the Whig Prime Minister Henry Pelham. The Onslows would have known both these influential gardens and they may have looked to them for inspiration. Lady Onslow, wife of the 3rd Baron, Sir John Evelyn and friends dined in the Cottage (one of the ornamental garden buildings) at Claremont in June 1750. The Duke of Newcastle's gardener took the guests 'four Dishes of Fruit which were very fine; apricocks, Strawberries, Rarspberries, & Cherries' and reported to the Duke that 'they were very much pleased'.

James Seymour's c.1750 view of the west front shows the new, more informal style of planting adopted near the house

James Seymour's painting of the west front of the house c.1750 gives a glimpse of this new, more informal style of gardening adopted close to the house. To the south of the house, the long terrace was landscaped to soften its formal lines and then planted with informal clumps of mixed trees. These clumps included fir trees, which were highly fashionable at this date, both for their rarity (many new trees were being introduced from America) and for their associations with ideas of classical landscapes and 'arcadia', as shown in the paintings of Claude. The formal pool and its fountain were transformed into 'a fine grotto of shellwork', which was sunk into the hill to the south of the house. Grottoes became popular in the 1740s, particularly with advocates of the informal garden landscape who were inspired by the poetry of Alexander Pope. The parterres on the east side of the house were removed and replaced with lawn. The fore-

court to the house remained unchanged (it was probably laid out by Leoni himself), but the avenue of trees leading to it was felled and the edges of the neighbouring groves were softened, to give the approach a more naturalistic appearance. In August 1747 the new garden was visited by George Vertue, who commented on the 'fine Views & Visto's' from the house and on 'the park & walks noble Great and delightfull'. Despite the informalisation of the garden near to the house, many formal areas of the garden remained unchanged, suggesting a reluctance or inability to spend the large sums of money required to develop the entire pleasure ground.

The next major change to the garden came after 1776, on the succession of the 4th Baron, George Onslow (later 1st Earl) – Surveyor of the King's Gardens and Waters during the 1760s – when John Willock made a survey of the garden and estate at Clandon. Mr Willock of New Burlington Street in London was the land agent who auctioned 1,511 acres of Lord Onslow's Surrey land in July 1778.

The survey was probably intended to inform Lord Onslow about his inheritance (it shows that most of the land surrounding Clandon was tenanted) and it may have been designed to show to prospective gardeners. The garden had changed remarkably little since the 1720s, and by this time must have appeared very old-fashioned. No action was taken until 1781, when the 4th Baron's finances, which had been shaky, allowed him to call in 'Capability' Brown to look over the garden and suggest changes. Brown was nearing the end of his long and distinguished career when he drew up plans for the garden. He improved the entrance to the estate by designing new lodges (incorporating the existing, fine early 18th-century gates attributed to Jean Montigny) and – long overdue – the demolition of the Tudor stables, which still stood within feet of Leoni's Palladian house. The new stables, to Brown's own design, were put up at Temple Court, out of sight with other ancillary buildings.

Brown swept away all the formal elements in the garden that had survived since the time of the 1st Baron. The canal was transformed into a lake, avenues were felled (though he preserved selected trees to form clumps) and he removed hedges and fences in order to make the area outside the pleasure garden into a large park, uninterrupted by boundaries. Despite the emphasis on the wider landscape, it is likely that Brown included flowering shrubberies close to the house, but the finer points of his work have since been lost, as his plan of Clandon has not been seen since 1927. The effect of the changes to the park and garden are recorded in a description of 1792, when the planting would have been established, if young: 'The park affords a rich pasture and is plentifully stocked with deer. In the pleasure-ground a romantick neatness prevails, where art and nature mutually support each other.'

After Brown had worked his magic, neither the 2nd nor 3rd Earl appears to have been moved to make changes to the garden. Although the 3rd Earl chose not to live at Clandon, the garden was apparently kept up. The kitchen garden was in operation, the adjoining orchard was producing large quantities of apples, and there was a nursery for young trees. The 3rd Earl's gardener at Clandon Regis (his pile of a house in West Clandon) was Edmund Eldridge, who had worked there from at least 1841 until the 3rd Earl's death, when Eldridge received the large legacy of £320 10s. Eldridge may have also had responsibility for the pleasure ground at Clandon, as it was found in 'a fair state of preservation' on the succession of the 4th Earl in 1870.

Although only seventeen, the 4th Earl immediately took the garden in hand and transformed it. He looked for advice to the artist and landscape gardener William Andrews Nesfield, who first visited in January 1871. The young Earl's diary recorded the meeting: 'Nesfield said that the place might be made very nice if a certain amount of money laid out ... many trees might be cut down and vistas cut through the wilderness also all the bushes in front of the house might go.' Nesfield paid a second visit the next month, when he made sketches of the pleasure grounds and walks, and proposed paths be made on the south and east sides of the house. Nesfield also marked out areas to be planted with trees, including one 'near the canal in order to hide the ugly corner of the pond.' His suggestion that the pleasure ground (presumably a series of shrubberies laid out by Brown) to the east of the house should be laid to lawn, was also adopted.

Activity in the garden carried on apace, and not a year passed without some major work or innovation taking place. Hot-houses and a peach house were built in the kitchen garden. Hundreds of trees were planted on the estate, and particular attention was paid to 'plugging gaps' to shield the house from the Guildford road. In 1876 the double Cranley Avenue of copper and common beech was planted before the west front of the house in celebration of the birth of the 4th Earl's first son Richard (later the 5th Earl). This was typical of the 4th Earl, who had a strong sense of family and felt that his work at Clandon was to be enjoyed by future generations. Tom Butler, an old Clandon retainer, remembered when a youth planting 'stripling limes which were to replace the elm trees that lined the drive. The elms would be felled, so the 4th Earl told the young Tom, before his grandson still unborn, reached his majority.' A gift of 30 deer from Lady Grantley of Wonersh Park saw them in the park for the first time in many years. Despite the reintroduction of deer, increasing amounts of the park were fenced and used for grazing cattle. By 1897 the view from the house of open parkland created a hundred years before by 'Capability' Brown had been lost.

After the initial flurry of activity, development in the garden slowed down in the 1880s and stopped whilst the 4th Earl and his family were in New Zealand. However, after their return in 1892, the gardens changed enormously, with large areas previously lawn or park being cultivated and taken into the garden. The 4th Earl appears to have taken the lead in matters horticultural; he kept a garden notebook and diary and was clearly a knowledgeable plantsman. He was not above getting his hands dirty and spent time in the glass-houses propagating and making cuttings. His notebooks record horticultural successes and failures, plants to buy, those to move and ideas for the improvement of all areas

of the garden. The 4th Earl swapped plants with other keen gardeners, including the 2nd Duke of Westminster and Ellen Willmott, the first woman member of the Linnean Society and renowned for her garden at Warley Place in Brentwood, Essex. He drew inspiration from other gardens both at home and abroad. Kew was a regular haunt, as was Wisley. The 4th Earl was also a regular at London flower shows, where he went in search of new ideas and the latest introductions. It was at shows like those held at the Horticultural Halls, the Temple and Holland House that he placed orders with nurseries, some from as far afield as Japan.

With so many influences, the gardens at Clandon contained a mix of traditional plants (particularly in the more natural areas) and new introductions and tender plants (often cultivated during the winter in glass-houses). Plans for the garden were drawn up,

The Formal Garden in 1925

but it is not known who was employed to advise after Nesfield's death in 1881. The garden adopted elements of the informal style popularised by William Robinson and Gertrude Jekyll. They rejected the formal bedding-out of plants and urged a more artistic and naturalistic approach to flower gardening based on colour, often drawing inspiration from English cottage gardens. Their influence was reflected in the Bulb Lawn, the Iris Walk and the herbaceous borders. The expansion of the garden was reflected in the number of gardeners needed to maintain it; H. W. Blake, appointed Head Gardener *c.*1890, was assisted by Under-gardener Sydney Sayer and between eight and nine other gardeners and labourers. Mr Blake was exceedingly proud of the many thousands of primulas he raised for the 4th Earl's Primula Dell. He would also have been responsible for arranging the plants (including palms) and flowers in the house. Cutting beds in the kitchen garden provided flowers for both Clandon and the Onslows' London house at Richmond Terrace. When the Onslows were in London, produce and flowers were sent up by train three times each week from Clandon.

The newly developed areas included the Maori House garden (see p. 53), the Iris Walk, pergola, Bulb Park, lily bed, Bamboo Walk and Dutch Garden. The 4th Earl was extremely fond of irises, planting a 250-yard-long Iris Walk next to the lake, which was his 'especial delight and hobby' and often photographed by him and his younger son, Huia. As reported by the *Gardeners' Chronicle*, the 4th Earl had 'procured all the finest varieties ... as representative as any in these islands'. In 1905 1,000 Spanish irises were added to the walk, and the 'legion' of other iris varieties included 'Princess of Wales', 'Madame Chereau', *sibirica*, *reticulata* and *orientalis*.

Nearer the house, a pergola was built linking the east lawn with the Dutch Garden. The pergola (based on one seen by the 4th Earl in Rome) was planted with a great variety of roses. The rambler 'Dorothy Perkins' was interplanted with 'Félicité Perpétue', and other climbers included 'Carmine Pillar', 'Queen Alexandra', 'Jersey Beauty' and *wichuraiana*. While the roses were at their best in early July, other climbers ensured the pergola was colourful throughout the season with clematis,

hops, annual convulvuli (probably Morning Glory) and virginia creeper. The narrow bed at the foot of the pergola was planted with lilies, polyanthus, forget-me-nots, *nicotiana* (tobacco plants) and Japanese anemones.

Wild areas of the garden, such as the Primula Dell (with little streams of water running through it) and the Wilderness, were planted with thousands of primulas, daffodils, aconites, snowdrops, hellebores and trilliums (no mean feat, considering the chalky soil). There were more unusual bulbs planted in the Bulb Park and Lawn, including colchicums and the 'latest narcissi ... double white poeticus'. The 4th Earl also planted beds of flowering shrubs and trees such as tamarix, daphne, azaleas, rhododendrons and *Magnolia stellata* (some imported from Japan). Lady Onslow's only obvious contribution was her 'Aromatic Garden', which was, by 1910, the only formal area of planting at Clandon, showing that the Countess had not kept up with gardening fashion to the same extent as her husband. The *Gardeners' Chronicle* praised the scented plants, including roses, lavender and southernwood (*Artemisia abrotanum*), and conceded that the 'plants utilised are of sufficiently free-growing habits to prevent any severe aspect'.

The last major development carried out by the 4th Earl came in 1901, with the building and planting up of the Dutch Garden. This sunken garden, which lay on the edge of the garden near the church, was modelled on the Pond Garden at Hampton Court Palace, which Mr Blake visited in 1901, and plans were drawn up by George Jackson & Sons. 'It has a pool in the centre, and the borders are occupied by bold groups of handsome flowers, whilst specimens of clipped plants are dotted over the grass.' The topiary consisted of birds, urns and capacious armchairs, ranged about the pond.

The 5th Earl did not inherit his father's passion for gardening, and after returning from the First World War he faced difficulties in keeping up the gardens. Lack of manpower and the need to cut down expenditure gradually led to areas of the garden being let go. In 1924 the 5th Earl saved from demolition an Ionic Temple designed by William and Henry Inwood in 1838 for the 3rd Earl's garden at Clandon Regis (described by the 4th Earl as 'absurd'). The temple was re-erected by the lake, where it can be seen today. The kitchen garden was leased – an arrangement which was far from satisfactory – the Onslows feeling that the fruit and vegetables provided for their table were of poor quality, whilst the 'first class' produce went to market for the gardener's profit. During the Second World War, the east and south lawns were ploughed up in support of the 'Dig for Victory' campaign. Chickens were kept, and much-needed vegetables were tended by the Blakiston family (who lived at Clandon from 1942 to 1945) and Viscountess Cranley. James Lees-Milne commented in his diary on the 'hideousness of the surrounding grounds, for there is no garden'. He continued: 'Trees have been allowed to grow right up to the front door so that the main elevation (which faces the wrong way and gets no sun) cannot be seen from a distance. A screen of revolting conifers has been planted as a windbreak against the only elevation that could otherwise have been seen.' After the death of the 5th Earl at the end of the Second World War, his son, the 6th Earl, and his family returned to Clandon. The much-admired

Bulb Park became an opportunity for raising income. The 'daffodils that took the winds of March with beauty were daily picked from the bulb park by the gardeners until early May'.

Lady Iveagh's generous gift of Clandon in 1956 included only seven acres of immeditate garden and the Merrow Lodges – the wider park remained in the ownership of her nephew, the 6th Earl. By this time only a fraction of the 4th Earl's garden was regularly maintained, though some areas survived, albeit in a wild state. The pergola had long since gone, and the Dutch Garden, largely forgotten, had become rather like the 'Secret Garden', visited only by adventurous children such as Caroline Blakiston. In the early days, Pamela, Countess of Onslow supervised the gardens and chose cut flowers for the house – an important link which gave the house a more 'lived-in' feel for visitors. The gardens continued to be maintained, but were neither returned to their appearance in the 4th Earl's time, nor were they developed in new ways, as the National Trust lacked the necessary funds to create a new garden.

As the house benefited from the generous

The small formal garden planted beneath the south front by the National Trust

bequest of Mrs Gubbay, so did the garden. In 1971 improvements to the garden were first considered by Graham Stuart Thomas, Gardens Adviser to the National Trust, and John Fowler, who had laid out his garden at St John's Hunting Lodge, Odiham, with impressive results. They agreed on only one point – that a small formal garden should be made beneath the south front, probably inspired by Knyff's view. This small garden was designed by Fowler, with horticultural expertise provided by Thomas and additional help from Paul Miles, and was laid out in 1976. This *palissade à l'Italienne* comprises boxed hornbeams and beds bordered by box. In the early 1980s the gardens, which appeared rather mean in relation to the house, were given a boost by the replanting of the Dutch Garden. The plantings were loosely based on those found there in the 4th Earl's time, but the effect achieved is much the same. A large herbaceous border was planted on the north side of the east lawn, later followed by a smaller one on the south side, this has New Zealand plants to complement Hinemihi.

THE GROTTO

First seen in Seymour's painting of the west front of Clandon, the Grotto with its dense backdrop of evergreens was probably built in the early 1740s by the 3rd Lord Onslow. This simple form of grotto is built of flint, brick and tufa to imitate rusticated stone. Broken wine bottles are embedded in the ceiling – an unusual material that was perhaps intended to throw coloured light into the Grotto.

At the rear of the Grotto is a small plunge pool, with steps down into the water. This may have been used, but it seems more likely that it was intended to conjure up Virgil's imagery in the *Aeneid*: *Intus aquae dulces, vivoque sedilia saxo, Nympharum domus* ('Within, fresh water and seats in the living rock, the home of the nymphs'). These words adorned the grottoes at both Stourhead and The Leasowes, and were probably intended to convey an ambience of classical mystery. The Grotto at Clandon was originally filled with sculpture. Each of the five niches once contained a head after the Antique. Now only three – Pan, Zeus and Poseidon – survive, but these add to the atmosphere

of antiquity. A plaster cast of *The Three Graces* after Canova used to stand at the entrance, but has been removed for conservation and will be displayed inside the house.

HINEMIHI

'One of the curios brought back from New Zealand by my father is a Maori whare.... I believe it is the only thing of its kind in Europe, or indeed, outside of New Zealand, and it is a very fine specimen.' So wrote the 5th Earl of Onslow about 'Hinemihi o te Ao Tawhito' (Hinemihi of the Old World), an extremely rare building with an important place in Maori culture.

The *whare* (meeting house) was the focus of village life in Te Wairoa, a small community in the shadow of the Mount Tarawera volcano on North Island. Since the 1880s the New Zealand government had promoted immigration, and the area had become popular with tourists. The nearby town of Rotorua was developed as a spa resort complete

The carved doorway of Hinemihi, a Maori whare (meeting house)

with sanatorium. Intrepid visitors were encouraged to explore local sights including the Pink and White Terraces rising out of Lake Rotomahana (formed by silica dissolving in natural hot springs), New Zealand's '8th Wonder of the World'. The Maori settlement at Te Wairoa (which had been somewhat anglicised by missionaries) also became a tourist attraction, where visitors were welcome to mix with locals, stay in one of its two hotels, and spend money.

Aporo Wharekaniwha (d. 1886), head of the Ngati Hinemihi sub-tribe and an entrepreneur, decided to enhance the visitor experience in Te Wairoa. He built a new meeting house, which would, for a small fee, allow tourists to take part in Maori culture. Aporo named his *whare* Hinemihi after a 16th-century chief who was primarily remembered for her enormous pet lizard named Kataore, and it was unlike any other *whare* before (or since). Its painted decorative panels were carved from the traditional totara wood by two local artisans, Wero Taroi and his young pupil Tene Waitere. The carvings represent Maori myth, legend and history and have deep spiritual significance. The *whare* is a sacred place, where ancestral spirits dwell and protect their descendants. Aporo embraced European ideas, and so Hinemihi did not have the traditional reed roof, but one made from totara shingles. The final touch was for Aporo to set gold sovereigns and other coins into the carvings of Hinemihi, in place of the more usual shells, earning it the nickname 'House with the Golden Eyes'.

Hinemihi was completed in 1881 and it served both as a traditional meeting place for the Maori community and a venue for tourist shows. It was a great success with some tourists who enjoyed watching the Maori dancing and the staged ceremonies within. However, others were less impressed: 'Excited by the rum and pakeha [European settler] approval, the dancers often bring their haka to a pitch of indescribable indecency. There are innocent hakas ... but at Te Wairoa these innocent ones are more frequently exceeded than not, and the result is often unlimited drunkenness and immorality.' One tourist noted that at Hinemihi there was 'a brief ordinary dance ... [or

one] complete with its indecencies, which they said gentlemen usually preferred ... the miserable people are paid to disgrace themselves...'. In time, Hinemihi's notoriety spread and it became a famous landmark, appearing on postcards and souvenirs.

The party in Te Wairoa came to an abrupt end at 1.30am on 10 June 1886, when Mount Tarawera erupted, covering its slopes and the village with red-hot rock, ash and mud. The majority of buildings in Te Wairoa caught fire or collapsed under the weight of the debris raining down. About 100 villagers and tourists died where they lay in bed or were killed by the falling stones as they fled outside. Years later, Aporo's son Mika recalled that night: 'Many of us sought for safety in Hinemihi. The house was filled with people. The weight of volcanic dust and ashes was so great on the roof of Hinemihi, that several of the heke [rafters] snapped. We had to put up stays to keep the roof from caving in upon us.' Hinemihi was one of only two buildings left standing after the eruption. Hinemihi was half-buried, forcing the 50 or so survivors to dig their way out through the hot sludge. The entire area had been devastated, and so the inhabitants, who had lost their homes, possessions and livelihoods, dispersed to other regions. Hinemihi was abandoned but not forgotten; Mika Aporo returned to find that 'some pakeha had taken various parts of Hinemihi away as souvenirs ... at least three large carved slabs had gone'.

In January 1892 Hinemihi was brought to the attention of Lord Onslow, who was nearing the end of his term as Governor and had been looking to buy a *whare*. Roger Dansey, the Post Master at Rotorua (who conducted the deal on Lord Onslow's behalf), secured the 23 pieces of carving for £50 from Mika (the money to be divided amongst Mika, Tene Waitera and others who helped to build the *whare*). Dansey also had the foresight to have each piece of carving numbered and a plan drawn up of their positions, complete with instructions for reassembly in England, and a brief history of the *whare*.

Hinemihi arrived at Clandon in April 1892, was reassembled near the lake as a summer-house, and given a roof of traditional thin reed thatch rather than shingle, as it had had at Te Wairoa. Hinemihi was surrounded by its own garden: the meeting house was framed by *Iris virginica* and *versicolor*, and its roof was covered by a 'Crimson Rambler' rose. The bank behind Hinemihi was planted with scarlet oriental poppies. The 4th Earl's gardening diary for June 1909 recorded that 'The Maori House garden's one of the most effective things this year.'

Hinemihi was to make one last move, to its present site underneath an oak tree on the east lawn. Many New Zealand soldiers fought in Europe during the First World War and some were admitted to Clandon (which was a hospital), where Hinemihi must have been a reassuring sight. Apparently concerned about its condition in the damp soil by the lake, Maori soldiers, assisted by others, rebuilt and reroofed the *whare*.

Hinemihi has been restored twice since: in 1978, when it gained the thick thatch roof it has today – an error arising from looking at photographs of the *whare* when it was covered with ash after the eruption of Mount Tarawera – and in 1995, after it had stood at Clandon for more than 100 years. Members of the Ngati Hinemihi, who had visited Clandon in 1986, were particularly keen to restore the front wall, which had been removed, probably in the 1930s, and move some of the carvings, which

had been fixed wrongly in the past. As luck would have it, some missing carvings were found in the attics at Clandon and could be returned to their rightful place on the *whare*, but there remained some gaps. This new carved work was carried out by Colin Tihi, a descendant of chief Aporo Wharekaniwha and Robert Rika, great-great-grandson of Tene Waitere, from totara trees felled near Mount Tarawera. The carvings were presented to the National Trust to commemorate its own centenary in 1995, and a totara sapling was planted next to Hinemihi to mark the occasion. Hinemihi ensures the continued close relationship between the Ngati Hinemihi in New Zealand, the Ngati Ranana (the London Maori group), the London Kohanga Reo (Maori language school for children) and Clandon. Ngati Ranana and Kohanga Reo hold their annual *hangi* at Hinemihi. Prayers are said and then a traditional meal of pork or mutton, kumara and pumpkin and bread stuffing is cooked in the *umu*, an oven made in a pit and heated by hot rocks. The National Trust has benefited enormously from the skills and knowledge of traditional craftsmen to preserve Hinemihi for Maori and *pakeha*.

Hinemihi on the morning after the eruption of Mount Tarawera

THE ONSLOW FAMILY
FROM EARLIEST TIMES TO 1740

'The Seat is Old, and the Estate is Old too,' wrote Daniel Defoe of the first house at Clandon – spectacularly painted by Leendert Knyff in 1708. This 'fine Seat here, under the Downs', or the core of it, was bought by Sir Richard Onslow (1601–64) in 1641 from his Surrey neighbour Sir Richard Weston III (1591–1652) of Sutton Place. Sir Richard was the grandson of Richard Onslow the 'Black Speaker' (1528–71), who founded the Onslow family's fortunes in Surrey during the 1550s by marrying a local heiress, Katherine Harding, and setting up house at her seat, Knoll or Knowle (near Cranleigh). The Onslow (or de Ondeslowe) family are recorded from the 12th century and later became Lords of the Manor of Onslow near Shrewsbury in the Welsh borders.

Humphrey Onslow (1497–1573) was a prominent guildsman and civic leader; holding office successively as Bailiff of Shrewsbury and High Sheriff of Shropshire. His younger brother Roger (1498–c.1538) (father of Richard the Black Speaker) was Warden of the Mercers, Ironmongers and Goldsmiths Company in Shrewsbury and moved to London to further his interests in the wool trade. Taking his family to London enabled both his sons, Richard the Black Speaker (so called because of his swarthy appearance), and his elder brother Fulke (d. 1602) to establish political careers. Fulke became Clerk to the House of Commons, and the Black Speaker (MP for Steyning in Sussex), after showing considerable ability at the Bar, was given by Queen Elizabeth the perpetual lease of Shrewsbury Castle and the use of Blackfriars Convent (which became his London house). In 1566 he was appointed Solicitor-General and later that year was elected Speaker of the House of Commons, the first of the Onslows to hold this post. At first, Richard had attempted to refuse the appointment, making several excuses (including pleading the 'barrenness of

his own learning'), none of which was accepted by the Queen or Parliament. The House of Commons sat for only a short time, during which Richard had to mediate between MPs, who were anxious to clarify the Queen's marriage and succession, and the Queen herself, who wanted 'no further talk of that matter'. The Queen grew so tired of the MPs' discussion of these topics that she 'suffered five years to elapse' before summoning Parliament again, by which time Richard had died of a 'pestilential fever' caught in 1571 whilst visiting his uncle, Humphrey Onslow, in Shrewsbury. His tomb in the abbey church, Shrewsbury records that he was 'of good stature, most agreeable mien, grave

Sir Richard Onslow (1601–64), 'The Red Fox of Surrey', who bought the Clandon estate in 1641

Jacobean Clandon, as depicted in Knyff's bird's-eye view of 1708. It was demolished to make way for the present house

voice, eloquent, most studious of truth, the treasure of every virtue, sincere, liberal and incorruptible'. A cartouche bearing the Black Speaker's arms can be seen in the Marble Hall.

The Black Speaker's grandson, Sir Richard, probably purchased Clandon more for the 1,000-acre estate than for the 'hunting lodge' that stood there, as Sir Richard Weston III was well known for his skills in agriculture and husbandry. Weston cut the Wey Navigation from Guildford to the River Thames in order to improve trade – a costly undertaking which forced the sale of the Clandon estate to the Onslows. Sir Richard Onslow was knighted by James I in 1624 and had, according to his great-grandson Arthur (the Great Speaker), 'great spirit and abilities, very ambitious and ... a sort of art and cunning about him'. Such was his slyness that Oliver Cromwell called him the 'Fox of Surrey'. Sir Richard was a Parliamentarian who raised a regiment and besieged Basing House in support of the Roundhead cause. He aroused Cromwell's suspicions and was forced to retire to Surrey after he refused to carry 'things to extremities against the King' and had arrived too late to

help Cromwell in the pursuit of the Royalist army at Worcester in 1651.

Although described early on as a hunting lodge, the Westons' Clandon would have been lavishly decorated. Sir Richard Weston I (1465–1542) accompanied Henry VIII to the Field of Cloth of Gold in 1520 and had seen on his travels in France Renaissance ornamentation which he later introduced to his house at Sutton Place. Clandon may well also have had similar decoration, some of the earliest of its type seen in England. In 1542 the hunting lodge at Clandon had seven principal rooms, including a great chamber, a 'doble presse chamber' (with tapestries, a table carpet and a leather chair) and a Chapel with 'alter clothes of tawney velvat wt the crucyfyxe of Criste and yor armes apon them'; this reveals that the Weston family were Roman Catholic recusants (forced by Henry VIII, and later Elizabeth I, to worship in secret). This first building was probably swallowed up by extensions at the beginning of the 17th century: it is likely to have been part of the north side of the house (as shown by Knyff), as this building appears to have the spiral, double chimneystacks characteristic of Tudor architecture.

Clandon, as bought by Sir Richard Onslow some hundred years later, was an impressive house. Its

Dutch-style gables, its clock and turrets, its large windows and E-shaped plan had much in common with the so-called 'prodigy houses' of the early 17th century, such as Blickling Hall, Norfolk, and Hatfield House, Hertfordshire. The galleried court-yard at Clandon was reminiscent (though on a smaller scale) of the early 17th-century Stone Court at Knole, Kent, which was built alongside the Great Hall and provided a sheltered walkway from one side of the courtyard to the other. Nothing, save for the movement of the clock that once surmounted the roof, and the hour bell, survives of the house. The clock was put to use, probably in the stable block, and was, when they were demolished, installed in the stables 'Capability' Brown built in the 1780s.

In common with many other Tudor and Jacobean houses, the domestic offices (including stables) at Clandon were adjacent to the house. These two large courtyards would have housed horses, carriages, stores and workshops on the ground floor. The attic floor above, with its small, dormer windows, would probably have accommo-dated outside servants (grooms, gardeners) and lower status indoor servants (laundry staff, foot-men). At the north-west corner was a laundry and next to it, a drying ground, where clothes were laid and hung out to dry. This range of buildings survived Leoni's rebuilding of the house in the early 18th century, but was demolished during the 1st Earl's improvements, probably in the late 1780s.

Sir Richard Onslow continued to live at Knoll until his death in 1664, 'by some hurt ... he received from lightning', whilst his eldest son, Arthur (1622–88), set up house at Clandon. Arthur's first wife, Rose, died in childbirth in 1648, but he married Mary Foote a year later and they lived at Clandon with their growing family (they had eight children between 1650 and 1664). Mary was the daughter and co-heiress (with her sister Sarah) of Sir Thomas Foote, Lord Mayor of London, whose baronetcy reverted to his son-in-law, Arthur Onslow, on his death in 1688. Sir Arthur's youngest brother, Denzil (1640/1–1721) of Pyrford Court, married Sarah Foote (widow of Sir John Lewis, Bt), thus capturing the entire Foote fortune for the two Onslow brothers.

Sir Arthur was, like his father and grandfather, MP for Surrey and served as a JP with his father in Guildford. As an important Surrey Whig, Sir Arthur was implicated in the failed Rye House Plot to assassinate Charles II and his brother, the Duke of York (later James II). Clandon was searched and the arms found there confiscated. He was charged with dissent, and his Tory opponents, including James Gresham, hoped 'to abate the influence of the Clandon Satans over the West end of this County'. Despite the fines imposed, this was only a tem-porary set-back to the rising Onslow family: Sir Arthur retired to Clandon to devote his energies to his enthusiasm for fish and fishing. Sir Arthur corre-sponded with the diarist John Evelyn on the subject and they swapped fish to improve their stocks. Sir Arthur was bequeathed '200 best carp' and appointed 'overseer of his fishponds' by a neigh-bouring squire, Anthony Smith, such was his knowledge of the subject. His grandson, also Arthur (the Great Speaker), said of him that 'he was hospitable, generous and very charitable to the

Sir Arthur Onslow, 2nd Bt (1622–88), who was an enthu-siastic angler

poor' and that he took great delight in hunting at Clandon. His charitable acts, which included contributing to the building of both the Town Hall and Grammar School library in Guildford, gained the Onslow family popularity, political influence and votes. When Sir Arthur died in 1688, his 'funeral was attended by such a concourse of people' that 'the train of people who followed his hearse, in coaches, on horseback, and afoot, held from Clandon almost to Guildford', which apparently caused James II to take umbrage. On her death, his wife Mary left all her furniture at Clandon to her grandson Thomas (the future 2nd Lord Onslow), apart from her 'purple bed', which she bequeathed to her favourite granddaughter, Mary Reeve.

THE 1ST LORD ONSLOW

Sir Arthur's eldest son, Sir Richard (1654–1717), later 1st Baron Onslow, 'Improv'd and Beautify'd both the House and the Estate too very much' and commissioned Knyff to paint his panorama of it in 1708. The 1st Lord Onslow's improvements to the house were probably confined to interior decoration and furnishings, as there appear to have been no new extensions made to the house. He probably also laid out the extensive formal gardens, which were on a par with those at Badminton, Gloucestershire, and Hampton Court, Herefordshire. A bowling green to the south, conveniently next to the house, was surrounded by parterres, ornamental pools, fountains, avenues and a wilderness garden. Rides led out from the house into the deer-park and fields beyond. Minor repairs to the house at Clandon were recorded in the 1st Lord Onslow's account book, including a payment in 1704 to 'ye carpeters for altering ye hall at Clandon £4 7s 4d' and in 1706 £4 5s was paid 'for ye Marble chimneypieces', though it is not known in which rooms these were installed. Work was often given to local craftsmen who supported Lord Onslow and his brother Foote (1655–1710) in elections, including the glazier Richard Puttock (1705).

This activity reflected the rise in importance of the Onslow family, confirmed by Defoe's report

Richard, 1st Lord Onslow (1654–1717) in old age. He laid out extensive formal gardens at Clandon

that 'The House has several times been Honour'd with the Presence of both King William and King George'. The patent that conferred Lord Onslow's peerage in 1716 stated that our 'well-beloved counsellor ... has so far raised the lustre of his family, which has been continually increasing during a long succession of his ancestors and will transmit the fame to his heir (a person not unworthy of his birth)'. The 1st Lord Onslow was a zealous Whig who was lauded 'to the skies' by his party, but derided by the Tories, who named him 'Stiff Dick' on account of his rigorous enforcement of Parliamentary procedure. Lord Onslow spent many years in public service: MP for Guildford, Lord of the Admiralty, Privy Counsellor and Chancellor of the Exchequer (1714–15). A staunch supporter of the Hanoverian succession, he fought (and won) a duel against Lewis Oglethorpe MP, who was suspected of Jacobite sympathies. Lord Dartmouth described him as 'a very trifling, vain man, of a ridiculous figure'. Queen Caroline confirmed his appearance, but was more forgiving of his char-

acter: 'Notwithstanding the plainness of his coun-
tenance and person, there was something *great* in his
manner and carriage that drew a a particular respect
to him as soon as he was seen.' 1708 was a defining
year for Lord Onslow: he was voted Speaker of the
House of Commons, the second of his family to
hold this office, and his son, Thomas, married the
heiress Elizabeth Knight.

The Clandon State Bed dates from *c.*1710 and
would have stood in a suite of state rooms imposing
enough to receive royal guests. The 'noble and
costly Bedstead' (as it was described in the 1778
inventory) may have been made in the hope that
Queen Anne might visit Lord Onslow (who gave
the Commons address to the Queen on the death of
her husband, Prince George of Denmark, in 1708).
The bed and its suite of furniture would have been
the most important, precious and expensive pieces
of furniture in the house. They are apparently the
only pieces to have been kept after the demolition
of the house and the building of the new house by
the 2nd Baron, although the Mortlake tapestries of
The Twelve Months (Saloon) may also have come
from the first house. Unfortunately, the inventory
that Lord Onslow instructed to be taken on his
death has not survived, but in his Will he
bequeathed to his wife Elizabeth 'all ye bedding,
glasses, cabinett, chest of Drawers, tables, chaires &
furniture in or belonging to ye chamber where in
we now lye at Clandon or in her owne closet,
together with ye plate belonging to her dressing
table'. The remaining furniture, including the State
Bed, was bequeathed to his son, Thomas, 2nd Lord
Onslow. Lady Onslow was said to have been so
distressed at the death of her husband, that she
threw herself into the pond at the Archbishop's
Palace at Croydon and was drowned.

THE 2ND LORD ONSLOW

Thomas, 2nd Lord Onslow was born in 1679 and
was described 20 years later by Evelyn as a 'very
hopefull Gent'. In 1697 he accompanied the
English ambassadors to The Hague during the
negotiations for the Treaty of Ryswick, and probably went to Paris in 1698 with the Duke of
Portland, Ambassador Extraordinary to Louis XIV.

*Thomas, 2nd Lord Onslow (1679–1740), the builder of
Clandon*

This suggests a far from parochial outlook, and
may – at least partly – explain his bold decision to
commission a fashionable Italian architect to
rebuild Clandon. He was 'a very successful debater',
both in the Commons and, after 1717, in the House
of Lords, holding various Court and County posts
(Out Ranger of Windsor Great Park, 1715–17, an
office which thereafter became a family sinecure;
Lord Lieutenant of Surrey and High Steward of
Guildford, 1717–40). He was something of a
favourite of George I and II, the former being
extremely concerned when Onslow was shot and
severely wounded by a madman while returning
from fox-hunting near Guildford in 1723. Due to
Onslow's intervention, his assailant was spared the

death penalty. His cousin Arthur Onslow left the most complete account of his character:

He was not without parts and spirit and some knowledge of the world, and had a notion of magnificence suited to his rank and fortune, but had such a mixture of what was wrong in everything he thought said and did, and had so much of pride and covetousness too, that his behaviour, conversation and dealings with people were generally distasteful and sometimes shocking, and had many bitter enemies but with not very few friends (to whom he was not unkind).

His 'notion of magnificence' was certainly enhanced by his marriage in 1708 to Elizabeth Knight, 'a *West-Indian*, a Lady of a large Fortune', according to the antiquary John Aubrey. As the heiress to her father and uncle – both Jamaican merchants with considerable property in Jamaica and England – her fortune was popularly estimated at £70,000, a vast sum that ensured 'great competition for her hand', as 'the greatest heiress of her time'. Speaker Arthur Onslow described her as 'a woman of the truest goodness of mind and heart I ever knew' – a favourable opinion that is consistent with the apparently amiable character of her full-length portrait. The Will of her uncle, Charles Knight, described her as his 'beloved niece', who – among other assets – was to receive slaves (both in the Jamaican plantations and 'on the high seas in transit'). This presumably explains the presence in the Marble Hall of two marble busts of blackamoors over the principal doorways. Her money did not go only into bricks and mortar, for her husband also bought land in Surrey (around Guildford and Woking) and in Sussex. His close association with the nascent insurance market may also have been made possible by the Knight fortune.

In 1720 Lord Onslow became the first Governor of the Royal Exchange Assurance Corporation, which originated in a subscription (1717) 'for raising the sum of one million sterling, as a fund for insuring ships and merchandize at sea'. Lord Onslow was among the 286 contributors, and it is possible that the value of his holdings was greatly increased during the stock market boom of 1719–20, when 'Onslow's insurance' stock doubled between January and February 1719. In 1720 Royal Exchange Assurance shares began the year at £18,

Elizabeth Knight, who married the 2nd Lord Onslow in 1708. Her inheritance paid for the building of the house

reached over £200 in August, but had plummeted to £8 by December. We do not know whether Onslow was able to profit from this meteoric rise before the collapse of the so-called 'South Sea Bubble'. But it is not unlikely that he did, especially as his cousin, Speaker Onslow, criticised his capacity for 'covetousness'. That Clandon was rebuilt in the 1720s suggests that successful speculation may have been a contributory factor. Indeed, the Onslows' finances continued to be healthy for another 50 years.

Elizabeth Knight died of smallpox in 1731. According to Speaker Arthur Onslow, she 'died much too soon for everybody that stood in any relation to her'. Lord Onslow died nine years later.

THE BUILDING AND PURPOSE OF CLANDON

Clandon's architectural distinction is that it was designed by an Italian architect, Giacomo Leoni (c.1686–1746), who published the first English translation of Andrea Palladio's *Quattro Libri dell' Architettura* (1555). Like Palladio, Leoni was from northern Italy and describes himself as a Venetian on the title-page of his edition of Palladio, which appeared in instalments from 1715 until 1720. Given that Palladio had been idolised by English connoisseurs since the early 17th century, Leoni's publication would have ensured his own status among contemporary English patrons and fellow architects. However, very little is known about him, or about his comparatively few English commissions. Only a handful of his buildings survive today, of which Clandon is the most complete, retaining much of its interior decoration. There is no documentary evidence for Leoni's responsibility for Clandon, although the attribution was made as early as 1760, when Horace Walpole noted that the house was 'built by Leoni for the 1st Lord Onslow;

very magnificent, but rather wanting taste than in a bad one'. Appended to Leoni's 1726 translation of the famous architectural treatise by the 15th-century Florentine, Leon Battista Alberti, is a list of Leoni's works, and engravings of some of them, including a design for an urban bridge, dedicated to the 2nd Lord Onslow. However, Clandon is not included and its date remains a matter for conjecture, although Daniel Defoe declared that it was 're-edified' before 1724, and Frederick, Prince of Wales was apparently entertained in Leoni's new house in 1729. It has been argued that Clandon's omission from Leoni's *Alberti* suggests a date later than 1729 (the date of the latest plate in Leoni's book), but Clandon is not the only house to be omitted. Neither Lyme Park, Cheshire, nor Moulsham Hall, Essex, designed in 1725 and 1728 respectively, were included.

Why and when did the 2nd Lord Onslow choose to rebuild his family house and to place the commission in Leoni's hands? The answer is that we

The entrance front

shall probably never know. None of the relevant documents apparently survives, either for the commissioning of Clandon or for its construction. Nor do we possess any of the personal papers of the 1st and 2nd Lords Onslow, so their own thoughts on the matter are unknown, and the earliest inventory of Clandon is 1778, so there is no record of the original furnishing of the house. Leoni had come to England via the cosmopolitan court of the Elector Palatine in Düsseldorf, where the Court architect, Count Matteo d'Alberti, was strongly influenced not only by Italian architecture, but also by English Palladianism, especially the works of Inigo Jones. Through d'Alberti, Leoni probably became an anglophile before he set foot in England.

Leoni's earliest designs for an Englishman were alternative proposals (1715) for the rebuilding of Wrest Park, Bedfordshire for Henry Grey, 22nd Earl and 1st Duke of Kent. Leoni also wrote a manuscript entitled *Compendious Directions for Builders* for the Duke about 1713. The Duke's family and the Onslows had a mutual connection with the Evelyns of Wotton, near Dorking. John Evelyn, the famous diarist and virtuoso, and his grandson, Sir John Evelyn, Bt, were friends of the 1st and 2nd Lords Onslow respectively. On 22 January 1699 John Evelyn the elder noted that 'Sir R. Onslow and his sonn (a very hopefull Gent) came to Visite me', as did in 1701 'the Earle of Kent' (the 21st Earl, father of Leoni's patron, the Duke). This could explain the employment at Clandon of a Venetian architect already in the orbit of the Kents. However, another Surrey neighbour, Thomas Scawen, was a patron of Leoni, who built a palatial house for him at Carshalton in 1722/3–7.

Given the prominence of the Onslows in parliamentary circles and in Society, Leoni could also have come to their notice in a myriad of other ways. Whatever the circumstances, it is clear that probably Sir Richard, 1st Lord Onslow, and certainly his son, the 2nd Lord Onslow, had a highly developed taste in architecture, and that the decision to demolish and rebuild the old house was taken at some time between Leoni's arrival in England around 1714 and certainly before 1733, the date on two lead hopper heads on the east front. There is a tradition, unsubstantiated by documentary evidence, that plans for rebuilding Clandon were already in place in 1713, four years before the 1st Lord Onslow's death in 1717. It has even been suggested that Leoni inherited a partially constructed building – a theory partly designed to explain certain unPalladian elements of the exterior. However, given the eclectic nature of Leoni's style – he was clearly influenced not only by Palladio, but by later Italian architects and by English architecture – this theory is superfluous (especially as there may have been subsequent, particularly late 19th-century, alterations). It is also unlikely that the 1st Lord Onslow, a man in his sixties, would have instigated such radical changes to his ancestral seat, despite Horace Walpole's 1760 statement to the contrary. Indeed, Speaker Arthur Onslow ascribed the building of 'the noble house' at Clandon entirely to the 2nd Lord Onslow, and both Aubrey (1718) and Defoe (1724) described what was evidently the old house, which the latter stated was 'Improv'd and Beautify'd' by the 1st Lord Onslow.

It is, however, not impossible that the idea of rebuilding Clandon came much earlier than the rebuilding itself. Something of the kind appears to have happened at Carshalton, where Scawen seems to have been fulfilling the terms of his uncle's Will, which required (in 1722) the rebuilding of the house 'as neare to and agreeable to the Modell I now have as may be'. The 1778 inventory of Clandon lists 'The Model of a Mansion, Cabinet and Frame', so perhaps both models were Leoni's. None of Leoni's plans for Clandon survives, but there is an unsigned and undated 'Plan of the New House', which appears to be a preliminary rough draft showing the rectangular outline of the house as built, surrounded by formal gardens, and a carriage sweep on the east front instead of the elaborate marble steps. This plan also indicates that the stable block and service buildings which flanked the old house were preserved to the north of the new one, which explains why there was so little provision made by Leoni for servants' bedrooms. The 'attic' or second floor was in fact a series of high, well-proportioned family or guest bedrooms, apart from those for a few personal attendants (such as lady's maids and valets).

The impetus for the demolition and rebuilding of the previous 'fine seat' must have been linked to several factors: the barony (conferred in 1716, as George I's first creation); a feeling that the family's nobility would be enhanced by an up-to-date and entirely fashionable building; a considerable interest in architecture; and, above all, the money to achieve these aspirations, through Thomas Onslow's marriage to the heiress Elizabeth Knight in 1708. This *annus mirabilis* also marked Sir Richard Onslow's appointment as Speaker of the House of Commons. It is perhaps no coincidence that 1708 is also the date of Knyff's panoramic oil painting of the old house at Clandon and its expansive formal landscape. Was it already in the Onslows' minds that this picture would record past grandeur, and that the Knight fortune would mark a new phase in the family's history?

THE EXTERIOR

Each of Clandon's elevations is different, betraying various influences. This variety was noted by Manning and Bray, the historians of Surrey, in 1804–14: 'the East front is in the English style; the West, where is the entrance by a double flight of stone steps, in the French style; and the South in the Italian.' The entrance façade on the west side is unusual for its panelled pediment reminiscent of James Gibbs's All Saints, Derby (1723–5). Leoni would also have known Matteo d'Alberti's Ursulinenkirche, Cologne (1709–11), as well as Venetian buildings by Jacopo Sansovino (whose Scuola Grande della Misericordia of 1532 may be the earliest use of the motif). Indeed, Leoni may have seen Sansovino's design for the 1532 Scuola in Lord Burlington's drawings collection, where it was then erroneously attributed to Palladio.

Since the addition in 1876 of the *porte-cochère*, the original effect of this façade has been seriously compromised. However, from James Seymour's painting (see p. 46), one can appreciate the intended balance between brick and stone (the brick quoins were clearly rendered in stone colour, thus framing the elevation), between the round-headed windows of the ground floor and those above, and between the rusticated and free stone in the central

The south front

pedimented frontispiece. The glazing bars were also much thicker than they are now (these were replaced in metal, possibly in the 1780s). Seymour's painting also shows that the forecourt was closed off by brick walls surmounted by dark-coloured railings on two sides, with an iron screen, painted white, in front, which presumably had in its centre the elaborate gates attributed to Jean Montigny, moved in the 1780s to the Merrow entrance to the park. Montigny came to England in 1710, so his gates could have been made for the old house at Clandon, but it is more likely that they were commissioned during the 1720s as part of Leoni's rebuilding. The forecourt arrangement was essentially the same as that for the old house at Clandon, depicted in Knyff's panoramic view, with the difference that the front door was reached via Leoni's elaborate double sets of marble steps and balustrades leading to a raised terrace. The concept of this 'Noble ascent in front [great] stone steps and balustrade', as Vertue described it in 1747, derives from Italian palace architecture, and was deliberately conceived as a prelude to the immense grandeur of the Marble Hall.

The landscape framing this forecourt appears to have been scarcely less formal than that depicted in 1708, and the entrance façade was still intended to be seen as the focal point of a long drive from the Guildford entrance to the park. By the time of

Seymour's view, the landscape had become more informal, but Seymour also shows that the stable yard and ancillary service buildings to the left (north) of the new house, are the same as those depicted in 1708. They were not to be demolished until the 1780s, when 'Capability' Brown rebuilt them well away from the house, near Temple Court. A photograph of the west front taken before the construction of the *porte-cochère* shows how this side of the house had looked since 'Capability' Brown's natural landscaping of the 1780s, with the grass sward of the park running up to the foot of Leoni's grand staircase and terrace.

The uncompromising mass of Clandon's rectangular block (and the east front in particular) is strongly reminiscent of Sansovino's Villa Garzoni at Pontecasale, near Padua. The south front, with its massive Corinthian pilasters, derives from Palladio's Palazzo Valmarana, but these Italian sources are filtered through English influences. As John Cornforth observed: 'the swags on both the south and east fronts belong to the Gibbons tradition which was scarcely dead when the house was building.' He also pointed out that Clandon is 'a curious fusion of Palladian and Baroque', drawing particular attention to the influence of Vanbrugh in the rows of round-headed windows and 'the consciously simple treatment of the arcading on the east side'. Leoni's debt to Wren, Hawksmoor and Vanbrugh is also evident in the finely pointed brickwork, whose preservation is an argument against the notion that some of the more eclectic elements of Clandon's architecture are due to later alterations. As Cornforth noted, 'there is no trace of alteration in the superb brickwork, which is so finely laid that it is difficult to disturb without leaving tell-tale signs'.

THE INTERIOR

The closest parallel to Clandon's interior decoration is Houghton Hall, Norfolk, also rebuilt in the 1720s. Several architects were involved at Houghton, and their patron, Sir Robert Walpole, the Whig Prime Minister, undoubtedly had considerable influence on the designs. For the interior decoration, William Kent was the prime mover.

Here, both in the ground plan and in the décor, there are direct parallels with Clandon. The placing of a double-height hall back-to-back with a saloon in the centre of the *piano nobile* is identical, as is the circuit of rooms around the perimeter. This arrangement was due to Colen Campbell, whose initial design for the rebuilding of Houghton is dated 1722, and whose Wanstead House, Essex (completed 1715), was a much-visited and admired example of a similar approach to planning, which derives from Inigo Jones. At Houghton, the full-height Stone Hall, with its monumental chimney-pieces and elaborate sculptural plasterwork, is very close to the concept of the Clandon Marble Hall. The same craftsmen were employed on both rooms: John Michael Rysbrack for the very similar chimneypieces (c.1728) and the Italian/Swiss *stuccadore* Giuseppe Artari for plasterwork. Artari was paid for the Houghton Stone Hall ceiling in early 1728, and, although he sometimes worked with his compatriot Giovanni Bagutti, the Houghton ceiling was his alone. The ceiling at Clandon is clearly by the same hand and is even grander, with whole figures in dramatic foreshortening, sprawling in Michelangelesque style around the huge expanse of the vault. This extraordinary composition – the most elaborate of its date in England – is inspired by Italian models such as the painted ceiling (begun 1597) of the Farnese Gallery in Rome by Annibale and Agostino Carracci. The central roundel of *Hercules and Omphale* is a direct copy after Annibale.

Similarly, Rysbrack's overmantel reliefs in the Clandon Marble Hall derive from Italian sources (in this case, Antique Roman), and that on the north wall is virtually identical to Rysbrack's later overmantel relief (c.1733) in the Marble Parlour at Houghton. Rysbrack's cartoon for the Houghton relief – a rare survival – is in the British Museum. Leoni is known to have worked with Rysbrack on at least one other occasion. The monument to Daniel Pulteney, cousin of William Pulteney, Earl of Bath (Sir Robert Walpole's political opponent), is signed by both Leoni and Rysbrack. The monument was presumably erected about 1732, when Pulteney's remains were moved to the East Cloister in Westminster Abbey.

The Stone Hall at Houghton Hall in Norfolk, which was created by the Onslows' political master, Sir Robert Walpole. It resembles Clandon's Marble Hall in many ways

These links with Houghton are a reminder of the 1st Lord Onslow's close political affiliation with Walpole. Both supported the Glorious Revolution and the Protestant Succession, and both were members of George I's Cabinet Council in 1714–15. In the latter year, Onslow was forced to retire due to ill-health, and Walpole succeeded him as Chancellor of the Exchequer. Onslow's son, Thomas, 2nd Lord Onslow, a Whig MP since 1702, became a Teller of the Exchequer in 1718 and served as such until his death. Both the 2nd and 3rd Lords Onslow were also political allies of Walpole, as was their cousin, Arthur, the Great Speaker.

Clandon seems, like Houghton, to have been conceived for the entertainment of large parties of friends, neighbours and the great. However, perhaps because Clandon is so near the metropolis, there are fewer bedrooms than at Houghton, where in 1741 they could 'make up at an hour's warning 110 beds'. Unfortunately, there is only one detailed account of how Clandon was used on ceremonial occasions in its heyday, but this indicates that it was possible to journey from London to Clandon and return the same day. On 27 May 1729, Frederick, Prince of Wales arrived at Clandon at one o'clock 'from Kensington [Palace] in an open Berlin [a form of carriage]'. On arrival, he 'dress'd himself' and then 'walked round part of the garden and into the Orangery in the midst of a Wilderness of greens'. On returning to the house, 'he went into the great room above stairs to dinner' with 40 guests,

including the Lord Chancellor, Peter King (a near neighbour at Ockham Park), two dukes and other dignitaries. The Prince 'satt at the upper end of a round table to which was joined a long one – on his left hand Ld Onslow satt. There were seven piramids of sweetmeats and fruit and 5 dishes between each and some dishes were charged [changed?]'. After dinner 'between four and five', the Prince spoke to Lady Onslow and the other ladies 'in the nexte room'. Then he 'mounted a grey horse' and went to the nearby Merrow races, where the winning horse won a '£100 plate' inaugurated by Prince Frederick's grandfather, George I. The Prince returned to Clandon and 'after drinking coffee and talking to Lady Onslow

Artari's plasterwork ceiling in the Marble Hall

and some of the circle of men took coach about seven and returned to Kensington – as he went off he bowed to Ld Onslow and said I thank you my Lord again and seemed well pleased with his entertainment'.

This indicates that Clandon should be seen – like Ham, Osterley and Syon – as a villa in the Roman sense, near the capital, but surrounded by a country estate, and designed for entertainment. The numerous accounts of life at Houghton suggest how Clandon might have been used and furnished. At Houghton, the ground floor, or basement, was dedicated to 'fox hunters, hospitality, noise, dirt and business'. Even though the lowest floor at Clandon is partially subterranean on three sides due to the rising ground, the rooms are high, and their function may have been similar. At both houses much of the basement was vaulted and stone-floored, and a central corridor ran the full length as a thoroughfare for family, guests and servants. At Houghton, and possibly at Clandon (although the precise use of all the rooms is unclear, due to the lack of an inventory), there were also dining rooms for breakfast and informal use, and rooms of business 'where tenants came to account'. The domestic offices and kitchen were also at this level, and at Clandon the kitchen was placed conveniently in the north-west corner, with a staircase adjoining, directly below the Speakers' Parlour, which Vertue described as 'a fine dineing room' in 1747.

It has always been supposed that Frederick, Prince of Wales was entertained on the second floor – in the room in the centre of the east front – on the basis that it was 'above stairs'. However, if one assumes that the lowest floor was also used, as at Houghton, by the family as well as servants, then the Prince would have dined, as one would expect, on the principal floor. This location for the Prince's dinner would have made much more sense, too, in terms of logistics. It would have been curious indeed if a room on the second floor so far from the kitchen would have been used, especially as there is no ceremonial staircase. Also, the so-called 'State Dining Room' on the second floor is plainly decorated – there is no stucco ceiling – and the chimneypieces are of the 1740s, which implies that

the room may have been unfinished in 1729. In the early 18th century, several rooms in a great house might have been used for dining. At Clandon, as at Houghton, the Marble Hall and Saloon would certainly have been used on occasions for the largest gatherings. The Speakers' Parlour, like the Marble Parlour at Houghton, would have been the room usually used as a dining room for important guests. However, Sir John Evelyn described a party of 'about forty' in 'the great roome'; therefore the most likely candidate – if not the Marble Hall – would have been the Palladio Room in the centre of the south front, overlooking the garden. Originally, this had direct access from the Marble Hall via the Oak Staircase Hall. Perhaps, however, the Prince entered it directly after his visit to the garden, via the set of stone steps. Access to the outside from the *piano nobile* was possible on three sides of Clandon, which suggests – as with the Prince's visit – that the links to the garden were considered aesthetically important as well as convenient.

The visitors' route through the house begins in the Marble Hall, which overwhelms by the scale and grandeur of the vast space (a 40 foot cube). Its Italian derivation – in terms of the architecture and plasterwork – would denote the fashionable cultivation of the owner, while the imagery in Rysbrack's chimneypieces and reliefs of hunting, grapes, flowers, produce and Roman sacrifice would have indicated hospitality, plenty and Clandon's situation amidst the country with its opportunities for sport, recreation and bucolic entertainment. From the Marble Hall, the 'processional' route is via the Saloon beyond: the two rooms are linked visually by the marble floor. However, it was also possible, via the four doors in the corners of the Marble Hall, to reach other parts of the house. The two main staircases – the Stone and Oak Staircases – are beyond the doors nearest the entrance door, while the two further side-doors lead, to the left (north), to the rooms on the north side and, to the right (south) to a passage that originally connected the Marble Hall with the principal state room – the Palladio Room – which fills the central three bays of the south front. The Marble Hall therefore fulfilled an important

Rysbrack's classical reliefs in the Marble Hall emphasize the theme of hospitality

practical function, given that all parts of the house, as well as the main and one of two secondary staircases, could be reached directly from it.

From the Saloon, the doors on either side led to two sets of rooms placed in *enfilade* around the circumference of the house (as at Houghton), an arrangement that allowed a complete circuit during large parties, but also for a gradual increase in the grandeur and status of the rooms. Thus on the south side, the Green Drawing Room (which retains its original block printed green wallpaper) gives on to the much smaller Hunting Room, which served as an ante-room to the most important room on this floor, the Palladio Room. Beyond the Palladio Room was another, smaller, drawing room – now called the Morning Room – and beyond that, the Oak Staircase Hall.

On the north side of the Saloon, the first room (now the State Bedroom) was the location of the State Bed by 1778; then (probably) came a dressing room (the present Onslow Museum), then the present Library, and, finally, the Parlour (or dining room), known since the early 19th century as the Speakers' Parlour.

Unfortunately, it is not now possible, as it is at Houghton, to understand the original uses of the rooms, and to appreciate how their decoration and contents served to establish their relative importance. We do know, however, that all the stucco ceilings were painted white, without colouring or gilding, and this would have enhanced their robustly sculptural character. At Houghton, several of the grandest ceilings were not stuccoed but elaborately painted in *trompe-l'oeil* Italian style by Kent, and so the treatment of the Clandon rooms was much less extravagant. This simpler approach at Clandon is also carried through to the wall decoration. Whereas at Houghton the walls were hung with textiles, at Clandon the rooms were either painted or hung with wallpaper (a cheaper, and comparatively new, alternative to silk and woollen damasks). The only exception – as far as we know – was that the Palladio Room was probably hung with the set of Mortlake *Twelve Months* tapestries, now in the Saloon. This would have enhanced the grandeur of the Palladian scheme described by Vertue, with its 'collums carvings ornamented richly'.

FROM 1740 TO 1870

THE 3RD LORD ONSLOW

Richard, 3rd Lord Onslow (1713–76) was educated at Eton and Cambridge. On his father's death in 1740 he inherited not only the peerage, but succeeded him as Lord Lieutenant of Surrey and High Steward of Guildford (a measure of the family's prominence in the county). In 1752, when George II was 'scattering ribands of all colours' before his return to Hanover that year, Onslow received the red riband of the Bath, presumably in recognition of his command of the Surrey Militia. Again, there is little evidence for a portrait of his character, and what little there is is somewhat contradictory. He was described by the waspish Lord Hervey as a 'Yes-and-No man', who spoke on one side and voted on the other. On 16 May 1741 he married Mary, daughter of Sir Edmund Elwill, 3rd Bt, of Egham. The marriage was not only childless, but apparently unhappy to the extent that Lord and Lady Onslow communicated only in writing, and at mealtimes a screen was set upon the dining table between them: 'Set the damned thing higher, you rascal', Lord Onslow is said to have roared at his footman, 'I can still see her face'. Such boorishness seems at odds with the assessment in Barlow's *Complete English Peerage* which appeared in 1775, the year before his death:

This nobleman's good nature and hospitality have had very disagreeable consequences: they induced his heirs to believe that he would by extravagance greatly prejudice his fortune, and he has calmly submitted to such regulations as were imposed upon him, whereby from being the proprietor of a very ample fortune he can now command but a very scanty pittance.

This suggests that his heir, George Onslow, son of his cousin, Speaker Arthur Onslow, had somehow arranged to protect his inheritance from Lord Onslow's extravagance (heavily ironic in view of his own). The 3rd Lord Onslow's economy drive seems to have been successful – the Clandon estate was worth £18,000 a year on his death, according to the *Gentleman's Magazine* in 1776. His previous excesses seem to have been connected with the Turf, the hunting field and associated entertainments. His racehorses, in particular 'Whynot' and 'Victorious', were legendary not only at Merrow Down – where a 'great Cock-Match' always followed the racing – but at Epsom and other courses. Lord Onslow is also said to have been something of a connoisseur, being described as a 'patron of the arts', and the purchaser of a 'magnificent Greek statue', which the 1st Earl of Onslow is said to have presented to either the 10th or 11th Earl of Pembroke, owners of one of the great 18th-century collections of Antique sculpture. According to Horace Walpole, Lord Onslow certainly bought (*c.*1762) the marble pillars of the Chapel at Audley End, Essex, and the antiquarian George Vertue noted in 1747 that Clandon was completed by him. This explains the elements of Clandon's interior decoration which seem to be later than Leoni's work of the 1720s, and not entirely in accord with his style – the plasterwork of the window reveals of the Library, for example, or the chimneypiece and overmantel in the Green Drawing Room.

Towards the end of the 3rd Lord Onslow's life a rather unsavoury series of letters was written to his heir, George Onslow, by the Rev. John Butler, the future Bishop of Oxford and Hereford. In June 1768 Butler wrote: 'We dined at Clandon last week, and had a more agreeable day than I expected. His Lordship was full of Conversation and very polite. He looked thin, and appears to have lost all Appetite.' By 1773, Onslow, who had recently recovered from an illness, was described by Butler as one 'who does great hurt by living and would benefit the world by dying'. This, of course,

The 3rd Lord Onslow was an enthusiastic patron of hunting and horse-racing on Merrow Down. This view, attributed to James Seymour, in the Green Drawing Room shows the grandstand where he entertained Frederick, Prince of Wales in 1729

was in the sense that George Onslow's succession to the title and estates was thereby delayed by 'that useless breath of his'. At last, on 8 October 1776, Lord Onslow died – 'My dear Lord, how happy I am to address you thus!' wrote the sycophantic Butler to the new (4th) Lord Onslow.

Whether the new Lord Onslow shared Butler's sentiments or not, he had been the heir apparent to Clandon since the death of his father, Speaker Arthur Onslow, in 1768, and was certainly short of ready money. In latter years, there had, apparently, been a coolness between the two lines of the family, both descended from Sir Arthur Onslow,

2nd Bt, who died in 1688. Their Whig credentials were equally impeccable, although the 3rd Lord Onslow was much less interested in politics than either of his two predecessors or Speaker Onslow and his son, George.

THE GREAT SPEAKER

Speaker Arthur Onslow was the third Onslow Speaker and, according to Manning, the Victorian historian of the office, was 'the best and purest who up to that period had ever presided over the deliberations of the House of Commons'. His beginnings were difficult, as his parents died young, leaving him responsible for the family and small estate. He was, however, taken up by the 1st Lord Onslow, treated as his 'second son', spending 'part of the summer for many years' at Clandon. Having been trained for the bar, he became secretary to his

The Great Speaker, Arthur Onslow, presiding over the House of Commons in 1730; by James Thornhill and William Hogarth (Library)

revered 'Uncle Onslow', on his appointment to the Chancellorship of the Exchequer. In 1720, with the backing of the 2nd Lord Onslow, he was elected MP for Guildford, and appointed Speaker in January 1727 during the premiership of Sir Robert Walpole. He was also Chancellor and Keeper of the Great Seal to Queen Caroline, George II's consort (the Purse of the Great Seal is at Clandon), and in 1734 he was appointed Treasurer of the Navy (a post he resigned in 1743 'from a feeling that it was inconsistent with the office of Speaker'). He held his beloved Speakership until 1761, when – in a moving ceremony – he was granted the thanks of the House 'for his constant and unwearied attendance in the chair, during the course of above thirty-three years, in five successive Parliaments'. Horace Walpole noted: 'He closed his public life in the most becoming manner, neither overacting modesty nor checking the tender sensibility which he necessarily felt at quitting the darling occupation of his life.' He was granted an honorarium of

£3,000 a year by the King, with reversion to his son, the 4th Lord Onslow, for life. Although he was occasionally lampooned for pomposity, for courting popularity and for bad temper (by Walpole and others), his genuine worth was justly expressed in George Grenville's valedictory speech in Parliament: 'Equally free from the sordid love of money, and from the dangerous taint of power, he was impartial to all, a constant encourager of rising genius, desirous to assist the most ignorant, and able to instruct the most knowing.' It was notable at the time that, despite the 'lucrative employment of Treasurer of the Navy', his income on retirement as Speaker was 'rather less than it had been in 1727, when he was first elected to it'. Probity and 'detestation of corruption' – rare attributes at the time – were among his principal virtues.

His 33 years as Speaker saw the introduction of proper records of parliamentary proceedings, as well as many procedures still current today. In retirement, Speaker Onslow encouraged the development of the British Museum, collected a valuable library (his bookplate was designed by William Kent – the copper plate is at Clandon) and a series of painted and engraved portraits of distinguished Englishmen. He corresponded with Horace Walpole about the history of British painting, and was consulted in 1733 by the Earl of Burlington on plans for a new Palladian rebuilding of the House of Commons. His collection came to Clandon as part of the 4th Lord Onslow's patrimony, but the majority was dispersed in the 19th century by the 3rd Earl of Onslow.

THE 4TH LORD AND 1ST EARL OF ONSLOW

The Great Speaker was idolised by his only son, the 4th Lord Onslow, who in 1769–70 copied into a book his father's 'Anecdotes and Miscellaneous Pieces' concerning the history of his family and of his own career. He commemorated him at Clandon by redecorating the Speakers' Parlour, and by placing over the Library chimneypiece the picture of 1730 depicting Speaker Onslow in the Chamber of the House of Commons with Sir Robert Walpole. He also created a family mausoleum in

Merrow church, transferring his father's remains from Walton-on-Thames, and erected a monument with a fulsome inscription in Holy Trinity church, Guildford. He was in no doubt that his father's distinction would be the 'greatest Honor' of the Onslows in 'future ages', stating that he 'admired his father when living, and shall to the last Hour of my Life feel and lament his Loss'.

The 4th Lord Onslow had already been elevated to the peerage in his own right a few months before succeeding to the Onslow barony. He was created Baron Cranley on 20 May 1776, and took his seat in the Lords the following day. His first speech in the Upper House was not until the following year, when he urged the discharge of the King's debts, and 'launched into encomiums of the personal and political virtues of the sovereign'. His adherence to the monarchy was certainly his principal route to

preferment and his eventual elevation to an earldom, but he was also a skilled political operator at a time when 'trimming' – or the ability to adjust one's opinions to the prevailing circumstances of the day – was the key to political advancement. As the scion of a distinguished Whig dynasty, Onslow was well connected from the start. He had entered Parliament in 1754 as MP for Rye in the interest of his father's and his own 'kind and partial' friend, the Duke of Newcastle, the then premier, whose niece, Henrietta Shelley, he had married the previous year. Newcastle (Prime Minister 1754–6 and 1757–62) was one of his first political mentors. Apart from politics, they shared an interest in good living, architecture and landscape gardening. Both were inordinately extravagant and decidedly uxorious (although Onslow was accused, in graphic terms, of infidelity and wife-beating in

In 1795 the 1st Earl was accompanying the King, when their coach was attacked by a republican mob; caricature by Gillray

1771). In 1786 Onslow acknowledged 'unspeakable obligations' to his wife, adoring 'her tenderness, truth, generosity, honour, real religion and integrity'.

In 1761 Onslow was elected MP for Surrey (his father's second constituency) and in July 1765 became a Lord of the Treasury in the Marquess of Rockingham's first ministry, despite his previous loyalty to Rockingham's rival, Earl Temple. This is one of several episodes in Onslow's career which suggests an eye to the main chance. His volte-face in 1769 from being a friend to an opponent of the radical John Wilkes is another example, which reduced his standing in Parliament and earned him the ridicule of the popular press. Some of this may have been due to Onslow's increasing prominence as a courtier, with its attendant requirement to vote in accordance with the wishes of George III. Onslow was Out-Ranger of Windsor Forest (1754–63), Surveyor of the King's Gardens and Waters (1761–4) – 'a very genteel office' according to Onslow – Comptroller of the Household (1777–9), Treasurer of the Household (1779–80) and a Lord of the Bedchamber (1780–1814). Like the 2nd Lord Onslow, who managed to maintain cordial relations with both George II and his hated son, Frederick, Prince of Wales, so the 4th Lord Onslow was friendly with both George III and the future George IV (even witnessing the latter's illegal marriage to Mrs Fitzherbert in 1785). In 1795, during the Bread Riots, he was in the royal coach when the King was on his way to open Parliament. The mob hurled republican insults and missiles, and Onslow himself recorded the King's sang-froid as, with the glass windows 'broken to pieces', he 'took one of the stones out of the cuff of his coat … and gave it to me saying, "I make you a present of this, as a mark of the civilities we have met with on our journey today".' On 1 June 1801, Onslow had an unexpected visit from the King, who rode up to his house on Richmond Green, and – in Onslow's own words – 'said he had determin'd to make me an Earl and had chose to be himself the first to inform me of it, and desir'd I would look upon it as a mark of his favour flowing from himself. He added that he had only one condition to make with me which was that I would not quit the

name of Onslow.' His patent as Earl of Onslow and Viscount Cranley is dated 14 June 1801.

At Clandon, the earldom was celebrated most tangibly by the redecoration and partial refurnishing of the Speakers' Parlour, with a painted scheme of oak graining incorporating earl's coronets above the doors. The new earl's full-length portrait in the so-called 'Windsor Uniform' inaugurated by George III – and still confined to the royal family and senior courtiers – replaced a portrait of George I over the chimneypiece. Otherwise, the 1st Earl's improvements at Clandon are rather earlier. The 1778 inventory, taken two years after his succession as 4th Lord Onslow, records the arrangement and contents of the house still presumably much as they were in the 3rd Lord Onslow's time.

The future 1st Earl seems to have turned his attention to modernising the house and park in the 1780s. This is curious, given that he is said to have been perilously close to bankruptcy in 1778. In January that year, the society commentator Mrs Delany wrote: 'Lord Onslow who was thought rich (and his lady had no reasons to think otherwise) is now declared to be an hundred thousand pounds in debt, and they feel so little shame, so little sensible of their folly and dishonesty, that they appear in the midst of all the numerous assemblies and spectacles as gay and as fine as ever.' Perhaps this is why Lord Onslow's friend, John Butler, was so exercised about the 3rd Lord Onslow's reluctance to die. It certainly explains the rapid sale of various assets, including much of the contents of Clandon (at auction in 1781), after Onslow's succession to the barony. Land was also sold, notably Speaker Arthur Onslow's house – Ember or Imber Court – and the manors of Esher and Thames Ditton. Despite this, 'Capability' Brown was brought in to lay out the park in a more natural taste and to demolish the stables adjoining the north front and rebuild them near Temple Court in the park. The house was also altered in fashionable style. The principal room – the so-called Palladio Room – was remodelled, and the Mortlake *Months* tapestries (now in the Saloon) were replaced by an elaborate French wallpaper designed by Réveillon: *Les Deux Pigeons*. Giltwood furniture – glasses and torchères in the most up-to-date mode of chaste Neo-classicism – was also installed. The ceiling was replaced in the Morning Room, which, like the Palladio Room, was also provided with a Neo-classical chimneypiece.

These alterations may have been instigated by Lady Onslow, who was not only 'of consequence and understanding', but also apparently a Francophile, which would explain the appearance at Clandon in 1791 of the Princesse de Lamballe, a friend of Marie-Antoinette, and a fugitive from the French Revolution. Clandon was also, by tradition, suggested in 1799 as a safe haven for Monsieur, the future Louis XVIII. Lady Onslow entertained Horace Walpole with titbits of society gossip, and in 1784, while on his way to see her at Richmond, he had his first sight 'at last' of an 'air-balloon'.

Lady Onslow died in 1802, and her husband's last years continued to be taken up with the routine of court duty in the years before the Regency Bill of 1811, as George III gradually sank into mindless decrepitude. Stewardson's portraits depict the Earl in old age, but the most perceptive image of him (probably in the 1790s) is the pastel by John Russell, who was one of the favourite portraitists of the Onslow family.

Onslow's reputation has tended to be clouded by his parliamentary machinations. He was described as 'a noisy, indiscreet man' by Walpole, and as a 'false, silly fellow' by the anonymous and vitriolic political commentator *Junius*. In the history of the Jockey Club (1792), there is a more balanced appraisal: 'As an arrant courtier we detest [him]; but as a man in social life, we respect and love him, as a person of the strictest honour and integrity; the best, the most indulgent of fathers; of unquestionable probity and liberality in all his private dealings.'

THE 2ND EARL

Lord and Lady Onslow had four sons (of whom two, Thomas and Edward, survived) and a daughter. Although there are few records of their family life at Clandon, Thomas (1754–1827), the heir, was certainly fond of his parents, requesting in his Will that his funeral should 'be conducted in the simple way that of my late father was – May God bless him and my Mother'. Thomas, who was given

Thomas, 2nd Earl of Onslow (1754–1827)

to outpourings of doggerel verse, corresponded affectionately with his father, often 'poetically'. In the family tradition, he entered Parliament, but as a Tory (which his father effectively became towards the end of his life), representing the family borough of Guildford (1784–1806). Never at a loss for words in his private life, his silence in the House of Commons remained unbroken. He was a Colonel in the Army and of the Surrey Militia, where he was described as 'quite an eccentric character' and 'a much better coachman than soldier'. Known as 'little Tom Onslow' on account of his short stature and his addiction to practical jokes, his most notable accomplishment was as a pre-eminent coach-driver at a time when it was the height of fashion for gentlemen to ape their coachmen. As he said:

I'm free to confess I should anxiously strive
Like a Lord to behave, like a Coachman to drive.

Towards the end of his life, he wrote an essay on the 'Sublime Art of Driving', declaring:

I deem myself without any arrogance whatsoever, perhaps one of the most competent men in England to

The 2nd Earl's passion for carriage-driving was satirised by Gillray in 1804

handle this subject; as it requires no talent, and because it would be difficult to find another man in all the British dominions who had been sufficiently idle and stupid enough to have driven four horses nearly every day of his life, for six or eight-and-forty years uninterruptedly! ... in short, every trick that could be played with 4 or 6 horses I have been fool enough to practice for nearly fifty years without one accident or one Rival!

According to Captain Gronow – one of the most entertaining memorialists of the day – 'Lord Onslow devoted his time to his stud, and being the master of four of the finest black horses in England, was always conspicuous in the parks'. He was, however, too eccentric even for the exclusive Four-in hand Club, 'for his carriage was painted black, and the whole turn-out had more of the appearance of belonging to an undertaker'. In 1804 he was caricatured by Gillray out driving, with the following verse:

What can Tommy Onslow do?
He can drive a curricle and two
Can Tommy Onslow do nothing more?
Yes, he can drive a phaeton and four

His 'buffoonery ... good temper and oddities' endeared him to many, and although he was 'destitute of any elegance of grace', he was 'most fluent in discourse'. Until 1790 he was a close friend of the Prince of Wales (the future George IV), who sometimes invited himself to Clandon on his way to Brighton. They both enjoyed racing (the Prince stayed at Clandon for the Guildford Races in 1786), but Onslow did not apparently share the royal taste for works of art. Soon after 1814 he sold the Prince a late 17th-century cabinet inlaid with hardstones – the one listed in 1778 in the State Bedroom (see p. 31), which is still in the Royal Collection. On a visit to Nuneham Park, Oxfordshire, in 1784, Onslow noted the 'furniture fit for Carleton House', the Prince's London palace, but then 'Grew bor'd with his [Earl Harcourt's] damned Guidos, Clauds, Vandykes and Boracios; and went to Oxford, where a good veal cutlet on a plate seem'd a much more rational object of admiration'.

Like his father, Tom Onslow was also popular with the King and Queen. His second wife, Charlotte Duncombe, whom he married in 1783, was Queen Charlotte's 'dearest Crany', a favourite lady-in-waiting. Four years older than her husband, she had been '*not* an afflicted widow' at the time of her engagement, which was announced soon after the death (at 26) of Tom Onslow's first wife, Arabella. The latter – according to her father-in-law – 'was moral, Conscientious and Religious.... Her person and Gentleness of Manners (for she was handsome, civil, elegant, cheerful, calm and composed at all times and in all places) made her admired wherever she went'. The children – three sons and a daughter – lived at Clandon with their grandparents after their mother's death.

Onslow's devotion to both his wives did not preclude his admiration of others. Mrs Bouverie, wife of Edward Bouverie, a friend of the Prince of Wales, was a particular favourite, not only because of 'the Loveliest and most perfect form' – Tom Onslow's words – 'that human nature cou'd produce', but also because she was 'the prettiest and easiest Horsewoman in England'. To Mrs Bouverie was dedicated one of Tom Onslow's masterpieces, unsurprisingly categorised by him as 'to be read by few': *The Bumfiddliad, address'd to Mrs Bouverie's Ass*.

Tom Onslow inherited the earldom in 1814 at 60. In his last years – a widower after 1819 – he lived mainly at Clandon, where he was a popular landlord, whose 'hand was always open' and who 'paid his tradesmen with the most regular punctuality' (a rare quality in those days). He opened up the park, taking delight in haranguing passers-by from the Library windows. His doctor, counselling moderation at Christmas, was met with the rebuke: 'Damn you, Sir: do you suppose that I don't eat a good dinner every day of my life!'

THE 3RD EARL

The 3rd Earl of Onslow, Arthur George (1777–1870), shared three characteristics with his very different father: he never spoke in either the Commons or the Lords and voted with the Tories; he was a versifier, dedicating a poem to the novelist Maria Edgeworth in 1811, with a typically unflattering final couplet:

While I'm well satisfied that all agree
My pen, like yours, Ma'am, can produce 'Ennui'

and he hunted with the Clandon harriers. At some time between 1818 and 1827 the mutual dislike between father and son erupted in an argument over the dinner table, and Arthur George moved out of Clandon for good. In 1818, aged 41, he had married Mary Fludyer, by whom he had a son, also Arthur George, and a daughter, Augusta. After the rift with his father, Arthur George bought Clandon Regis, the largest house in West Clandon, and made it even larger with flanking wings, while constructing temples 'containing plaster casts of some

of the most celebrated statues of antiquity' in the gardens. Here, in 1830, his beloved wife died. Her rooms were shut up, and many years later were found to be in a Miss Havisham-like state of suspended animation with 'even the piece of work on which she was engaged exactly as she had left it, and her needle sticking out of the reel of cotton'. Devastated by the loss of his wife, the 3rd Earl left Clandon Regis for Richmond. Clandon, which he had inherited in 1827, was shut up and by 1841 already had 'a forlorn and deserted air; most of the pictures and furniture having been removed'. Although the 3rd Earl was a popular landlord – he never raised the rents – repairs fell into abeyance, and the condition of the estate gradually reflected his neglect of the house. This may perhaps be partly explained by the death of his only son in 1856 at the age of only 36.

Among the 3rd Earl's first acts on inheriting Clandon was to sell the Great Speaker's collection

Arthur George, 3rd Earl of Onslow (1777–1870), who neglected Clandon

of historical portraits. The sale of the library (in 1841 still containing 'nearly all the works printed at Strawberry Hill', ie the product of Speaker Arthur's friendship with Horace Walpole) and other contents of Clandon was to follow after his death under the terms of his Will. By this time (1870) only his daughter, Lady Augusta, was still living, and she, the 3rd Earl's daughter-in-law, Viscountess Cranley, and her three daughters were the joint beneficiaries. The 3rd Earl is said to have loathed the idea of his property going to his nephew and heir, William Hillier Onslow.

All this would seem to imply that the 3rd Earl was an eccentric and bitter recluse. Such a caricature is all the more inevitable, when – as in the 3rd Earl's case – his private papers have disappeared and his public life was undistinguished. However, the redeeming feature in the 3rd Earl's case was a love of pictures and sculpture and, above all, his extraordinary patronage of Paul Hippolyte Delaroche (1797–1856), the French Romantic painter. In the early years of the 19th century, the future 3rd Earl had 'travelled' on the Continent, and, like many other Englishmen, had conceived an obsession with Napoleon Bonaparte. A marble bust of Napoleon is still at Clandon, although there were other portraits and relics in the 3rd Earl's collection. His commission to Delaroche was inspired by Jacques-Louis David's famous painting in the Louvre of *Napoleon crossing the Alps*. The 3rd Earl of Onslow found David's painting unrealistic and over-romanticised, and in 1848 – the year of revolutions – asked Delaroche to paint an historically accurate version. Delaroche's Napoleon is a subdued and thoughtful figure, his cloak fastened against the cold of the snow and ice, seated upon an Alpine pony led by a plodding guide. The painting arrived in England in 1850 and was hanging at Clandon in 1870, and after its sale in 1893, was presented to the Walker Art Gallery, Liverpool. The 3rd Lord Onslow's collection also included Old Masters as well as portrait busts, Sèvres china and French furniture.

The 3rd Earl's uncle, Edward (1758–1829), third son of the 1st Earl, founded a French dynasty of Onslows, some of whose portraits are at Clandon. Forced to leave the country due to a homosexual scandal in 1781, he repaired to Clermont Ferrand, where he quickly proposed to Marie-Rosalie de Bourdeilles de Brantôme. Her father, concerned lest his daughter would be lost to France, at first objected, but with Edward's father's help, a château was procured at Chalendrat near Vic le Comte in the Auvergne, and the pair were married in 1783. Edward Onslow took French nationality, and 'les Onslow' became known for musical, artistic and military accomplishments. Edward was imprisoned in 1789 during the Revolution, but released after his wife's direct application to the authorities. One of his sons served in Napoleon's Grand Armée and won the Légion d'honneur at the battle of Leipzig. This may explain the 3rd Earl's commission to Delaroche, who also taught the 3rd Earl's nephew, Edouard Onslow. Another of Edward's sons, George Onslow (1784–1853), was a composer of some note, sometimes called 'le Beethoven français', whose compositions earned him the notice of Schumann, Mendelssohn and Berlioz.

Napoleon crossing the Alps; by Paul Delaroche (Walker Art Gallery, Liverpool)

FROM 1870 TO 1939

THE 4TH EARL

After the death of his great-uncle in 1870, William Hillier Onslow, aged only seventeen, found himself the 4th Earl of Onslow and owner of Clandon Park. The inheritance was not a surprise, as Hillier's father, George, died unexpectedly in 1855, when his son was two years old, followed the next year by the 3rd Earl's only son. Hillier (as the 4th Earl was familiarly called) was brought up by his mother Mary (née Loftus, d. 1880), estranged from the 3rd Earl and his family. Arthur James, Hillier's Classics master at Eton, described him as 'pretty well the tallest, least embarrassed, and most self-possessed young man whom I had ever had the pleasure of meeting'. Hillier first visited Clandon on 2 November 1870, less than a week after the death of the 93-year-old 3rd Earl (he was not invited to attend the funeral), and recorded in his diary that 'the inside in very fair state of preservation considering its not been touched for 43 years' though 'all blinds, curtains, etc. had perished'. The stories describing Clandon as in a near-derelict state are exaggerated: grass was not growing up through the slabs in the Marble Hall, nor was the window glass broken, and nor was the place devoid of pictures and furniture. However, this should not diminish Hillier's hard work: 'What he achieved during the first ten or twelve years of his incumbency would have astonished those who afterwards enjoyed the profuse hospitality of Clandon.' Hillier was impressed by the Marble Hall ceiling and chimneypieces (which he knew to be by Rysbrack), the embroidery of the State Bed and Delaroche's painting *Napoleon crossing the Alps*.

Whilst the 3rd Earl lived first at Clandon Regis and later at Richmond, Clandon was looked after by Mary Dallen. Caretaker from at least 1841 (when she was recorded in the Census), Mrs Dallen was still living there, aged 73, on the arrival of the 4th Earl in 1870. Mrs Dallen lived with a young companion (either one of her daughters or her niece) in a small suite of rooms on the north-east side of the first floor (the Blue China Room was probably her sitting room), which were regularly decorated throughout these years. Gamekeeper Edmund Hook also lived in the house, presumably to help with heavy duties and to provide security. Mrs Dallen continued to carry out her tasks of lighting fires and opening windows until, aged 73, 'her strength failed her and she was compelled to discontinue'. Hillier soon took possession of the house, moving into the Library and 'Lady Harriott's bedroom and dressing room' above (Lady Henrietta or Harriott, wife of the 1st Earl). One of his first

William Hillier, 4th Earl of Onslow, who revived Clandon

visitors was Arthur James, who recalled that 'in descending the polished marble staircase in the Hall in our nailed boots [they were going shooting] we both slipped and tumbled down the treacherous steps side by side.'

Hillier began to plan the improvement and redecoration of the house, probably with the advice of his mother. In order to pay for the modernisation of Clandon and the many tenanted houses and farms (which had not been touched by the 3rd Earl and were now in lamentable condition), Hillier sold outlying land and property, benefiting from the new railway and Guildford's recent growth and prosperity. The most immediate practical improvements included installing central heating, connecting mains water and digging proper drains. At the same time he negotiated with his 'hated Aunt Augusta' over the Onslow heirlooms and remaining contents of the house:

She made me exceedingly angry by her pettishness. Nothing in the House worth having but Delaroche's Napoleon, Thorwaldsen's Shepherd, Canova's bust of Napoleon, and Hogarth's House of Commons, the latter I still hope to get hold of. Made me look at her absurd temple and strawberry beds.

Hillier was imbued with a sense of his family's history and it was a great disappointment to him that, by the terms of the 3rd Earl's Will, much of the family collection was bequeathed to the Earl's daughter Augusta, as they were not entailed. Aunt Augusta's collection (which included Onslow heirlooms) was sold at auction in 1893, and Hillier bought back many items, some of which can be seen at Clandon today: the pastels by John Russell of Onslow family members, the Worcester armorial dessert service (Speakers' Parlour) and the Louis XV *bureau à cylindre* (Palladio Room). Hillier was similarly sympathetic in his approach to the redecoration of the house. Instead of replacing the 18th-century silk *brocatelle* wall-hangings 'in ribbons' in the Green Drawing Room, he took advice and had them carefully restored in order to preserve the appearance of the room. He decorated the Speakers' Parlour with a specially made wallpaper in imitation of the early 19th-century paper probably hung there by the 1st Earl. The Library was entirely grained, probably by the 3rd Earl, but

Hillier preserved what would have been a rather eccentric and gloomy scheme. Upstairs, servant bedrooms, family bedrooms and nurseries were wallpapered, their names reflecting the patterns: Passion Flower Room, Rose Room, Bird Room (with Peacocks) and Pink Room. The majority of the rooms had red roller blinds at the windows. The Saloon is the most complete of his interiors to survive. In 1879 he had the walls covered with fabric, brought in the Mortlake tapestries, and had the room painted blue and cream, colours found in the tapestries. Hillier probably moved the State Bed into the room now known as the Green Drawing Room, and he and his wife Florence had their dressing room and bedroom in the Onslow Museum and the adjoining room (once again the State Bedroom).

The most obvious, and perhaps regrettable, change Hillier made was to build the *porte-cochère* on the entrance front, after a suggestion made by his landscape gardener, William Andrews Nesfield, that 'a very marked improvement might be made in the house by bringing the carriage drive on to a level with the top of the first six steps at the South [in fact west] front of the house'. The original flights of steps were found to be 'very inconvenient in wet weather'. The architect was George Devey (1820–86), who worked mostly in the vernacular or Jacobean styles, but in the 1870s he adopted a Georgian one. Leoni's original steps were moved forward and rearranged to make room for the *porte-cochère* and porch. The arch provided shelter for those arriving by carriage, and the porch provided a practical space for servants to greet visitors and for family to dispose of paraphernalia before entering the Marble Hall. The double set of doors also helped to keep the warmth in – a benefit not to be underestimated in a house as lofty as Clandon. Work was also begun in the garden, which had been somewhat neglected. A double avenue of copper and common beech was planted before the west front of the house to celebrate the birth of a son and heir in 1876, peach and other hot-houses were built at Temple Court and a tennis court laid in the Wilderness Garden.

All the work at Clandon did not prevent Hillier from pursuing other interests: he hunted and went

The 4th Earl photographing by Lake Rotoiti while Governor of New Zealand

shooting several times a week, acted in amateur dramatics (performing 'Chiselling' in the Palladio Room in 1874 to friends, family, villagers and Guildford worthies) entertained, played golf, took photographs and enjoyed listening to the gramophone. The Onslows liked to travel and spent three to four months abroad each year. Big game hunting, particularly in America, was a favourite pastime, and during his time most rooms at Clandon contained some trophy of taxidermy: a stuffed bear stood, full height, holding a tray (for drinks); bear, lynx, seal and buffalo skins littered the floor of the Marble Hall and the walls of the Oak Stairs were covered with mounted antlers. The house was always full of dogs: Hillier was a founder of the Battersea Dogs' Home, and the Onslows kept packs of dachshunds and basset-hounds. In 1887 *The World* reported, 'On a Buffalo rug which three years ago sheltered Lord and Lady Onslow while on their American travels, lies Nevski [a Russian poodle], ... Feo, a docile basset-hound, is in undisputed possession of a bear-skin.' Hillier's favourite dachshund was 'dear old' Waldy, his 'faithful companion at Oxford' and the 'greatest favourite both with Flo' and myself' (painting in the Onslow Museum). It was Hillier who introduced quarantine laws in an attempt to eradicate rabies from the British Isles. He was not without pluck, accompanying, at the drop of a hat, his friend Commander Van der Thann (1st Bavarian Corps) to the front during the Franco-Prussian War in 1871. Van der Thann said, 'Buy a horse and come along', and so he did. Mrs Onslow disapproved of her son's rash action: 'To get shot in your own country's quarrel was one thing, but to get shot in someone else's was without reason.' He returned only when forced by lack of money and his mother's refusal to send him more.

In 1875 Hillier married the Hon. Florence Gardner and began to take a more active part in local and national affairs. He became a Lord-in-Waiting to Queen Victoria in 1880 and received some friendly and useful advice from the Prime Minister, Disraeli: 'Always shut a door and always sit down when you get a chance.' Government appointments soon followed: Under-Secretary for the Colonies, Governor of New Zealand, Under-Secretary of State for India, Privy Councillor, President of the Board of Agriculture. It is as Governor of New Zealand that Hillier is best remembered. Appointed in 1888 at the age of 34, Hillier, Florence and their children Richard (Viscount Cranley), Gwendolen and Dorothy spent four years in New Zealand, leasing Clandon in their absence to the Blaines family. The Onslows were a great success in New Zealand, and their enlightened attitude helped to improve relations between the European settlers and Māori.

Whilst in New Zealand, Florence gave birth to their youngest son, named Victor Alexander Herbert Huia. His godmother, Queen Victoria, chose the first two names, his uncle, the third, and the fourth, Huia, was after the then rare (now extinct) native bird. For Hillier to give his child a Maori name (it also meant 'precious treasure') was more than an act of diplomacy, it was a gesture that recognised the importance of Maori culture. Always known as Huia, he was honoured as a member of the Ngati Huia group. Hillier described the ceremony to receive the ten-month-old into his group, complete with Huia feather in his hair :

The Nanny followed the Chief in a state of abject terror. After each nose rubbing, she tried to get him back, but the Chieftains only whisked him over her head and into the face of the next Maori lady. Strange to say, the kid never uttered a sound, but looked at the whole thing with an aspect of interested wonderment.

Huia had a great mind with wide-ranging interests: butterflies, moths and insects (his collection is in the Library), European folk songs, genetics, mesmerism, eugenics, photography and mountaineering. As a boy, Huia had a laboratory at Clandon and 'was always doing unaccountable things with chemicals'. He went up to Trinity College, Cambridge in 1909 where he read Natural, and later Mechanical, Sciences.

Huia's parents were equally lively, enjoying company and entertaining. From their marriage to Hillier's death in 1911, Florence kept a book in which was noted down their guests to luncheons, dinners, the regular 'Parliamentary dinners', 'Cabinet luncheons' (Hillier was Chairman of Committees in the House of Lords), after-theatre supper parties, children's tea parties, often accompanied by the respective menus. The 23 guests who dined on 6 May 1907 included the Prince and Princess of Wales (the future George V and his consort Queen Mary), the Lord Chancellor (Herbert Asquith) and many of the Londonderry House set. At Hillier's birthday dinner in 1883 six courses were served, including *Consommé à la Reine*, *Soles Colbert* and *Côtelettes d'agneau*. For many years the Clandon cook was a Neapolitan, Signor di Luca. Hillier loathed garlic, but occasionally di Luca would sneak a little into his cooking. If detected, this roused Hillier 'to fury' and he would 'pull out his pencil, seize a menu card and write "Bannissez l'ail de la cuisine" and send it forth to the kitchen.'

Huia Onslow

Though only in his late fifties, Hillier's health began to fail in 1910, and this 'good straight Englishman of the best type' was forced to retire from public life. Steps in the garden were covered with ramps so that he could continue to enjoy the flowers, plants and birds from his bath chair. A terrible shock came in July 1911, with the news that Huia had met with an accident whilst on holiday in the Dolomites. He had dived into Lake Misurina and had hit his head on a submerged rock. Despite numerous operations the accident left him paralysed. After a period of convalescence, Huia was determined to continue his studies so with the help of his nurse-cum-secretary Miss Moodie, he returned to Cambridge, where he began a serious study of genetics. To this end, he supervised the selective breeding of rabbits, noting down fur and eye colour. Consequently, Huia made very important discoveries in the study of dominant genes as illustrated by eye and hair colour inherited from parents, some of which form the foundation of contemporary genetics. He also made a large collection of butterflies, moths and other insects whilst carrying out a groundbreaking study of the iridescence on their wings. At the request of the War Office, during the First World War he investigated a method of detecting the distance of enemy gunfire during daylight. Again, his work was pioneering and led to the use of 'sound-ranging' detection on the battlefield. In 1919 Huia married fellow Cambridge academic Muriel Wheldale, continued to publish his findings in scientific journals, but died after a short illness in 1922.

Hillier's last journey was to visit Huia, in Hampstead. He died aged 58 in 1911 and was buried in the Onslow family vault at Merrow: English Maori sent a traditional rug as a pall to cover his coffin. A newspaper announced his death with the headline 'A full and laborious life'.

THE 5TH EARL

Richard, Viscount Cranley (the future 5th Earl) was born in 1876. He was, in later life, serious, studious and modest, writing in 1944, 'My career, though laborious, has not been distinguished, and my own humble achievements would hardly merit the trouble of record'. After Eton and a little travelling, Cranley went up to Oxford. Resolved 'to work very hard', his good intentions lasted all of ten days, and he was 'as idle as the idlest afterwards'. He gave his whole energies to amusing himself. His time was passed at luncheon clubs, playing cricket, hunting, polo and entering point-to-point meetings, and he had several trophies to show for it (on display in the Library). After cramming for his finals, Cranley got a Third in History and returned to Clandon to settle down, clear his debts (with help from his father), and decide upon a career.

Cranley started out in the Diplomatic Service in 1901, 'detailed for the meanest duties' in the Eastern Department of the Foreign Office. He was soon posted abroad: first to Madrid and Tangier, and then in 1904 to the British Embassy in St Petersburg, where he attended a Court Ball for 7,000 in the Winter Palace. According to Russian custom, Tsar Nicholas II came in last and 'wandered round the tables seeing that everyone had what they wanted to eat and drink; then he sat down anywhere'. He was in St Petersburg during

The 5th Earl of Onslow (1876–1945), who modernised Clandon

the March Revolution, but had little to report, other than watching 'troops moving about' and seeing 'churned up snow.... everything was quiet in the streets, but the whole town was full of rumours and stories and reports of the wildest character'. In 1906 he returned to England to marry Violet Bampfylde (daughter of Lord Poltimore), and the couple spent their honeymoon at Clandon before returning to St Petersburg. After Violet was taken seriously ill in Stockholm, Cranley was posted to Berlin to be nearer home. This was to be his last foreign posting. He returned to England in 1909 and retired from the Foreign Office after his father's death in 1911, when he took his seat in the House of Lords, and went into business in order to spend more time at Clandon and oversee the family's estates.

The 5th Earl had a great interest in the history of his family. He bought back Onslow family papers that came up for sale and organised them, chronologically, into albums. Knowing the Onslow history well, he undertook to write it up, drawing on the family's muniments. His history of the Onslows was objective and thorough and ran to nine typed calf-bound volumes, which formed the basis of C. E. Vulliamy's partisan work, *The Onslow Family 1528–1874*, published in 1953. The 5th Earl was President of the Surrey Archaeological Society and wrote many articles for the Society's journal on aspects of Onslow history.

In March 1913 the 5th Earl began a series of improvements at Clandon. Electric light, a new boiler and additional radiators were installed, and the domestic offices in the basement were decorated. A bathroom was plumbed-in for servants in the basement, situated in the corner of the Brushing Room (where boots, shoes and muddy hunting clothes were cleaned) and, apart from the coal cellar, the dirtiest room in the house. Work was probably planned for family bedrooms and the more important state rooms on the ground floor, but was not carried out until after the First World War.

Life changed abruptly at Clandon with the outbreak of war in 1914. The public-spirited Onslows offered Clandon as a hospital for injured troops. Lady Onslow had opened Clandon Cottage Hospital for London 'waifs' and so she was appointed Commandant, in charge of the Voluntary Aid Detachment working at Clandon and at two other nearby houses used for convalescence. The majority of rooms were cleared of furniture and used as wards, with some rooms on the second floor used to billet nurses. Lord Onslow's Dressing Room (now the Onslow Museum) was chosen as an operating theatre, because it had running water and an even north-east light. The wounded soldiers treated at Clandon came from the ranks and from all countries and usually arrived directly from the battlefield, 'shattered and half-starved'. There were 5,059 soldiers admitted and 747 operations were carried out. Some years later, Lady Onslow recalled that a young Canadian who had lost an arm was eager to help and 'seeing over the carved chimneypiece in his ward an old picture which appeared to him to require some cleaning, he proceeded to fetch a ladder ... walked up the steps with the intention of dusting the surface of the picture'. The unfortunate man lost his balance, put out his hand to steady himself, which 'went straight through the canvas'. He offered all the money he had – 6s 6d – 'to pay for that picture'. One night in October 1915 a German zeppelin flew over Clandon and despite the danger hospital staff went out and 'had a good view of it'. Lady Onslow recalled that 'during the firing [of anti-aircraft guns] and the dropping of bombs from the Zeppelin the whole house at Clandon shook and the windows rattled in an astonishing fashion.' There were no casualties, but there were 'great holes in the Portsmouth Road'.

The serious nature of some of the soldiers' illnesses and injuries and the epidemic of Spanish influenza during the winter of 1918 (which killed several patients and one VAD) meant that the hospital remained open until April 1919. On the discharge of the last soldiers to Woolwich, Lady Onslow was presented with a silver salt to commemorate her role and the use of Clandon as a hospital. The salt was acquired by the National Trust and can be seen in the Speakers' Parlour. In the early days of the war the 5th Earl helped organise the Red Cross operation, transporting and caring for wounded soldiers. He then signed up with the War Office as an intelligence officer. Whilst carrying out his job (which consisted of receiving intelligence reports and forwarding them to the appropriate department) he compiled all the office instructions and orders he received about the sending of communiqués, by pigeon and so forth. The orders were so numerous that they filled a book, which later became known to intelligence officers as 'Onslow's Bible'. The 5th Earl ended the war as Colonel in charge of censorship and publicity in France and was awarded the Légion d'honneur in recognition of his work. He returned to his political career after the war, becoming Under-Secretary of State at War, Privy Councillor and Chairman of Committees in the House of Lords (a position his father had held), whilst Violet spent increasing amounts of time at her brother's estate in Devon, because of her delicate state of health.

'Lady Gwendolen Onslow up a tree'. The 5th Earl's sister later helped to ensure that Clandon was saved for the nation

The Onslow family's ties with Guildford and Surrey were maintained by the 5th Earl, who was Lord Lieutenant of Surrey and a local magistrate. The 5th Earl was concerned by the lack of good housing in Guildford after the First World War and so formed a Public Utility Society to build a Garden City. Called Onslow Village, it provided good, affordable housing at low rents, which tenants were encouraged, in time, to buy (rather like a housing association). The 5th Earl sold 600 acres of land at Guildford Park Farm and Wilderness Farm to the Onslow Village Association at a quarter of its market value in order to provide suitable land near the centre of Guildford. In 1928 he donated six acres of Stag Hill on the outskirts of Guildford for the building of a new cathedral designed by Sir Edward Maufe for the growing town.

After the war, the 5th Earl again turned his atten-tion to making improvements at Clandon. Work was carried out by the Guildford firm Edmead & Sons and included the redecoration of many rooms, which must have looked rather tired after the hospital's occupation of the house. A new laundry room was installed in the basement, but Edmeads did not complete the work on time, which caused inconvenience according to the 5th Earl, 'as my clothes are being torn to pieces by the furious washing of the Steam Laundry' in Guildford. The *Country Life* photographs of the state rooms in 1925 show the house unchanged since the 4th Earl's time, but with much of the Victorian clutter and animal skins removed. The floor of the Marble Hall was covered with Indian rugs, though it was prob-ably no longer used as a drawing room. At some time between 1925 and 1941, the 5th Earl had many of the state rooms simply redecorated: his father's decorative schemes were probably thought to be rather fussy and detracting from the sculptural nature of the rooms. The Marble Hall was white-washed, including the marbling of the columns, which the 4th Earl had had painted in the 1870s. The tapestries were taken down in the Saloon and the figured wall-hangings removed to reveal the 18th-century panelling beneath. The entire room was painted white, including the overmantel, thus obliterating the 4th Earl's polychrome scheme, but unifying the room with the adjoining Marble Hall. The 1st Earl's Library decoration (which was *en suite* with the Speakers' Parlour) was treated similarly: the grained woodwork and ornamental plasterwork in the window embrasures and on the overmantel were painted white.

FROM 1939 TO 1956

'Clandon empty now you should requisition immediately or others will', telegraphed the 5th Earl in 1941 to the Director of the Public Record Office. Clandon had already been a billet for 20 evacuee children and their guardian, but this had not been a success. The accommodation (in the basement) was unsuitable because of damp, and so the children left for other homes in West Clandon. The 5th Earl was not apparently keen for the house to be used as a hospital, as in the First World War, but as a family historian and a member of the Government, he knew that the Public Record Office was looking for temporary homes for important state papers. The 5th Earl rightly thought that boxes of records would be a lot less trouble than billeted soldiers or a working hospital.

So the Onslows moved out of Clandon, and the remaining furniture was stored in the second-floor bedrooms, leaving the basement, ground and first floors clear for the Public Record Office. The PRO installed its Assistant Keeper, Noel Blakiston, his wife, the historian Georgiana Russell, and their two daughters, Rachel and Caroline, at Clandon in August 1941, along with Harry Pearce, a muniments clerk, and Bob White, an odd-job man who repaired documents. Charismatic, knowledgeable and enthusiastic about the arts, Blakiston was later a member of the National Trust Arts Panel. Cartons of records began arriving from Chancery Lane in October, and the delivery of the 300 tons of precious documents took some weeks. Boxes of deeds and case indexes were piled high in each

During the Second World War Clandon was used to store archives from the Public Record Office

The Blakiston family lived at Clandon during the Second World War. They are in the Morning Room

of the basement and ground-floor rooms, which were then sealed with Lady Onslow's personal lead seal marked 'VO'. Viscount and Viscountess Cranley (the future 6th Earl and Countess) with their two children, Michael (the future 7th Earl) and Teresa, moved into a cottage on the estate and made friends with the Blakistons. Lady Cranley, who was a nurse, helped to look after one of the Blakistons' daughters when she contracted scarlet fever in 1942, and the favour was returned when Michael caught measles. James Lees-Milne, Secretary of the National Trust's Historic Buildings Department, visited the Blakistons, 'sweet people' who were friends, in July 1942 and recorded in his diary that the 'house is dirty and in decay'. After tea 'Noel and the children gave a play in a toy theatre,

with scenery of Clandon made by themselves'. On a visit to Clandon the next summer, Lees-Milne was depressed by 'the soullessness of the house and the hideousness of the surrounding grounds, for there is no garden'.

During the hard winter of 1944, damp and burst pipes were a particular problem, and rats began to make a meal of some of the papers during 1945. Apparently immune to poisoned bait and traps, Blakiston ended up shooting the rats out of the Morning Room window. More dangerous to the house and its temporary contents was the threat of Nazi flying-bombs, as Clandon was directly under their flight-path. The spring of 1944 was the worst time: Blakiston, Pearce and White and their families were forced to live in the basement, whilst taking it in turns to carry out all night fire-watching. Bombs fell nearby, shaking the house and taking out windows, but thankfully little permanent damage was done. Victory in Europe on 8 May 1945 was marked by Caroline ringing the house bell. Celebrations were short-lived, as the 5th Earl died a month later. Pearce and White cleared the boxes of records from the Speakers' Parlour to make room for the Earl's coffin to lie in state for several days before his funeral in June 1945.

After leaving Winchester College, William Arthur Bampfylde Onslow, Viscount Cranley (1913–1971), son of the 5th Earl, worked his passage to Australia as a stoker on a merchant ship and once there took employment as a cattle rancher on farms in the bush. This romantic 'Boys' Own' life continued when he returned to England in 1931 to join the Life Guards. In 1938 he resigned his commission and followed his father and grandfather into politics. However, Cranley's political career was thrown off course by the outbreak of war in 1939. Shortly after, he joined the Territorial Army and spent the early part of the war as a Captain in the Western Desert. He was awarded the Military Cross in 1942 and later wrote *Men and Sand* about his experiences. He was given command of his regiment, the 4th County of London Yeomanry (Sharpshooters), and led them in the invasion of Italy. After landing at Salerno, they pushed north to Naples and fought on and crossed the Vulturno river near Caserta. Cranley was recalled to England with his regiment to prepare for the invasion on D-Day and the subsequent liberation of France. He was captured in the advance after only a week and spent the last months of the war in Europe in Offlag 79, a prisoner-of-war camp in Brunswick, Germany (his identity tags are in the Library).

Whilst away from home, Cranley's horses had to be destroyed because of the shortage of food; the inscribed hoof of the unfortunate 'Queenie' was used by him as a tie-pin cushion on his dressing-table (now displayed in the Library). In August 1945 arrangements were made by the PRO to accommodate Cranley, who had recently succeeded his father as the 6th Earl of Onslow and was keen to move back to Clandon on his return from Germany. The PRO cleared the Palladio Room and Hunting Room, and the Blakistons moved out of the Morning Room and their bedrooms on the east side of the first floor. Blakiston returned to

Clandon in March 1946 to supervise the removal of the hundreds of boxes back to Chancery Lane.

'How are the mighty fallen,' remarked the 6th Earl's elderly nanny when she visited Clandon after the Second World War. The 6th Earl and his first wife Pamela (d. 1992) continued to use a few rooms on the south side of the first floor. They abandoned the basement kitchen, putting in a bathroom and kitchen on the first floor. Their children Michael and Teresa had the run of the second floor, and they rented out two flats to help pay the bills. Lady Onslow recalled one tenant as 'a strange old gentleman from the Channel Islands ... with his large Pyrenean sheep dog – I was at pains to prevent the children questioning him closely on why he painted his face and dyed his hair.' The grand rooms on the ground floor were kept as family sitting rooms. This was a difficult time to make a large country house like Clandon comfortable for a young family, but the Onslows were determined to make a go of it, despite a backlog of maintenance, high taxation, a dearth of staff, the cold, lack of fuel and paucity of materials. After the war, many country-house owners found the task too daunting, and so their homes became schools or hotels, were divided into flats, or demolished. Although there were problems, and lack of money was usually first amongst these, the Onslows were happy to be at Clandon. Pamela, Lady Onslow remembered the family atmosphere at Clandon, particularly at Christmas, when 'immense logs burned in the hall fireplaces ... romantic and beautiful but marvellously ineffective' and a 'great tree was set in the middle of the hall'. On Christmas Eve there was a tea party, and the Onslows were joined by Lord and Lady

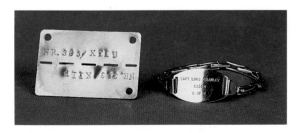

The identity tags of Captain Lord Cranley (later 6th Earl of Onslow), who spent the last months of the war in a German prisoner-of-war camp

Iveagh (the 6th Earl's aunt) and their grandchildren and staff and children from the estate and local farms. A sumptuous home-made tea was laid out in the Saloon and a conjuror performed tricks. Lady Onslow recognised that the family's possessions did not always represent the height of good taste, but the 'late Victorian furniture ... not very nice Indian rugs, Benares brass ornaments, stuffed birds and dreadful photographs of babies, and ... door stops made from favourite horses' hooves' were 'the glory ... of the Clandon that was Home'.

The 6th Earl's greatest passion was for ornithology (caged birds in particular), and he succeeded his father as President of the Royal Zoological Society. He built a large, heated aviary at Temple Court (Clandon's home farm) and kept many fancy birds in cages all over Clandon. One large cage was built of four iron bedsteads, sprayed gold, to house his favoured cockatoos. His first wife, Pamela, said that his love of birds was 'the delight of visiting children, the despair of his wife', presumably as they flew freely around the rooms. Scattered bird seed provided meals for their grandchildren's escaped mice and, worse, the rats that inhabited the basement.

In 1949 a crisis was reached, and the 6th Earl approached the National Trust for help. James Lees-Milne went to Clandon for tea with the Onslows to discuss the donation. Lady Onslow, he wrote in his diary, 'has excellent taste in dress and decoration, to judge by her appearance and the way she has reanimated Clandon after the mess she found it in.' Lees-Milne found the 6th Earl 'wearing attractively bizarre clothes, check tweed trousers, getting tubular towards the bottoms like the pilasters of Mannerist architects'. Before the gift of Clandon could proceed, the Onslows and other country-house owners were offered a life-line by Sir Ernest Gowers in his report, *Houses of Outstanding Historic or Architectural Interest*, which was concerned at the condition of many important houses and their collections. Gowers recommended that the government should give grants towards the maintenance of historically important houses on condition that they were open to the public. After 'a struggle, but a happy one', the Onslows moved out of Clandon to a house in the park, and in 1951,

Pamela, Countess of Onslow, with her son, Michael (the present Earl)

with advice from their friend, the local National Trust Representative, Robin Fedden, they opened the 'big house' to the public. Lady Onslow wrote the guidebook, both she and the 6th Earl showed groups round the house, and teas were offered in the old basement kitchen (now the shop). The Onslows overcame their fear of publicity and invited journalists to interview and photograph them, 'both of us smiling benignly with our children, giving little indication that the eighth governess had given notice that morning'. As Deputy Lieutenant of Surrey and High Steward of Guildford, Lord Onslow also offered the Corporation the use of the house for civic functions without charge. Despite the Onslows' continued efforts, it became clear that they could not manage and approached the National Trust once more. Lack of investment over many years meant that the house was in great need of repair: there was an attack of dry rot, leaking drains and a leaking roof – all to cost more than £24,000.

The saviour was the 6th Earl's aunt, Gwendolen, Countess of Iveagh (1881–1966). Lady Iveagh, eldest daughter of Hillier, the 4th Earl, spent her childhood at Clandon and served as her father's secretary until her marriage in 1903 to Sir Rupert Guinness, who succeeded his father as 2nd Earl of Iveagh in 1927. The Guinness family amassed an immense fortune from brewing, and their principal English house was Elveden in Suffolk, described by the author Augustus Hare as 'almost appallingly luxurious'. Both the 1st Earl of Iveagh and his son were great philanthropists, giving hundreds

of thousands of pounds towards slum clearance, workers' housing and medical research. The 1st Earl saved Kenwood House, Hampstead, and its collection for the nation in 1925 and the 2nd Earl gave his family's Dublin home, Iveagh House, to the Republic of Ireland in 1939. The 2nd Earl and his wife kept Pyrford Court, near to Clandon, a house built for them just after their marriage and named after Denzil Onslow's 17th-century house. Lady Iveagh became one of the first women MPs, after winning Southend-on-Sea in 1927, a seat she held until 1935. Lady Iveagh, with no doubt the support of her husband, saved Clandon from a very uncertain future. She bought Clandon and many of its contents from her nephew and then gave it to the National Trust along with an endowment to help preserve the house and contents. The 6th Earl also contributed towards paying the enormous repair bill that faced the National Trust. Once Clandon had been transferred to the Trust, Lady Iveagh wrote, 'It is with the deepest satisfaction that I can now feel that my old home is safe for the future.'

A Sèvres ewer and basin from the Gubbay collection

RESTORING CLANDON

By the late 1960s, the National Trust wished to improve the look of Clandon, which needed an injection of extra furniture and other contents to complement the rather sparse indigenous collection. The catalyst for a major reassessment of the house was the 1968 bequest to the National Trust by Mrs Gubbay of her fine 18th-century furniture, textiles and porcelain. With the additional benefit of a generous gift from Mr and Mrs Kenneth Levy to cover the cost of the collection's display at Clandon, the National Trust sought the advice of John Fowler on the redecoration and rearrangement of the rooms.

Clandon became something of a turning-point in the treatment of the National Trust's country houses, given Fowler's interest in trying to establish the previous decoration of rooms before deciding upon a decorative scheme of his own. His approach – with its use of 'scrapes' to identify the past history of a room's paintwork – looked forward to the current microscopic analysis of paint sections. However, it was inevitably much less accurate, and led – as we shall see – to certain assumptions that have since proved to be incorrect. Also, while the 1778 Clandon inventory was used as a reference point for upholstery and curtains, a shortage of funds led to compromises on the quality of the new materials. Sometimes the evidence was ignored in favour of a fabric that Fowler found attractive. He also introduced colours of his own to unify a room's palette. Thus the original plain white stucco ceilings of the 1720s had green, blue or grey added to their flat surfaces so as to tie up with the predominant colours of the wallpapers, paintwork or textiles. Fowler's approach at Clandon was not therefore scholarly or academic and should be seen as a personal reaction both to Clandon and to his brief to prepare it for the Gubbay collection.

MRS GUBBAY

Who was Mrs Gubbay, and how did her collection become indelibly linked with Clandon? When she died in 1968, her Will provided that her collection 'should not be dispersed after my death but should continue to be housed and displayed as a single collection under the name of "The Mrs Gubbay Collection" in some house belonging to the National Trust or if this should prove impracticable in the Victoria and Albert Museum.' In doing this,

Mrs Gubbay; painted by Rex Whistler (Blue China Room). Her collections now furnish Clandon Park

*Part of Mrs Gubbay's collection in her drawing room at
Little Trent Park*

she wished 'members of the public' to have an
opportunity to see what 'is recognised as being one
of the best private collections in this country'.

Mrs Gubbay was born about 1886 to E. D. Ezra
and Mozelle Sassoon, daughter of Sir Albert
(Abdullah) Sassoon, 1st Bt, a member of one of the
richest and most cultivated Jewish families, sometimes called the Rothschilds of the East, which
made a great fortune in the 19th century through
Indian, Far Eastern and Middle Eastern trade with
England. She spent her childhood in Bombay, but
the family also owned London palaces (her grandfather's was at 15 Kensington Gore). Through her
mother, she was the cousin of Sir Philip Sassoon, a
flamboyant patron, collector, host and politician,
who shared her interests, collaborating with her
on a pioneering and influential series of loan exhibitions held from 1928 to 1938 in his mansion in

Park Lane. Sir Philip's sister, Sybil, married the
future 5th Marquess of Cholmondeley in 1913, and
reigned as châtelaine of Houghton Hall, Norfolk,
from 1919 until her death in 1989. Houghton –
aptly enough, given its similarities to Clandon –
must have been an important element in defining
Mrs Gubbay's tastes. Mrs Gubbay and Sybil
Cholmondeley both acted as hostesses for the
bachelor Sir Philip. A close friend of the royal
family, and at the summit also of what Kenneth
Clark dubbed 'unstuffy, new world society', Sir
Philip Sassoon, according to Clark, was 'a kind of
Haroun al Raschid, entertaining with oriental magnificence in three large houses, endlessly kind to his
friends, witty, mercurial and ultimately
mysterious'. Mrs Gubbay is an equally enigmatic
figure, rarely mentioned in the reminiscences of her
contemporaries. While staying in 1934 at Port
Lympne, Sir Philip's villa on the Kent coast, Clark
was received 'by a small, dark, unprepossessing lady,
who gave her name as Hannah Gubbay, but did not

explain her *raison d'être*, which remained mysterious to the end. Even on a wet day the view over Romney Marsh from the terrace of Port Lympne is breathtaking and we admired it. Jane [Lady Clark] adding "It's so peaceful". "You won't find any peace in this house" said Mrs Gubbay in her sour, staccato, toneless voice.'

Mrs Gubbay displayed her collections at Little Trent Park, a house on the estate of Sir Philip's other country house, Trent Park, in Hertfordshire, and at her London house in Hertford Street. In 1972 Frank Davis remembered her London house, 'which, even then [in the 1920s], seemed to be filled to overflowing – one of those tall, narrow, houses which seemed even taller and narrower because the walls of both rooms and stairs were covered with the most splendid series of early 18th-century tall mirrors I have ever seen … The result was decidedly claustrophobic.' Little Trent Park was equally oppressive, 'an Aladdin's cave with pier glasses literally cutting into the ceilings and the rooms filled almost to bursting with cabinets of porcelain', according to John Cornforth and Gervase Jackson-Stops. The numerous photographs of the interiors taken soon after her death in 1968 reveal a plethora of symmetrical arrangements based upon chimneypieces, side-tables, mirrors, cabinets and beds, around which there were patterns of sconces, plates, porcelain plaques and the famous oriental porcelain birds upon giltwood wall-brackets.

According to Davis, Mrs Gubbay acquired her pieces mostly in the 1920s and '30s, two decades that saw the break-up of numerous ancestral collections. Unfortunately, however, there are few records of her various acquisitions, so their earlier provenance is often unknown. She was 'very knowledgeable indeed and delighted to share her knowledge – and her prejudices – with anyone who had the sense to listen':

She was a familiar figure in Bond Street, often accompanied by Queen Mary [consort of George V], and, together with a few others in a similarly enviable financial position and with similar tastes, must have been a godsend to antique dealers during the years following the Wall Street collapse at the end of the 1920s…. Her interests in furniture were confined almost wholly to 18th-century England though she did own one or two excellent French pieces, and she appreciated the best satinwood from the last decade of the century no less than the discreet walnut of the reigns of Queen Anne and George I.

She also collected lacquer, giltwood and gilt gesso furniture – again predominantly of the early 18th century. Mrs Gubbay was doubtless encouraged by scholars like Christopher Hussey and Margaret Jourdain, but it is important to remember that she (and her friend Queen Mary) enjoyed shopping, and that much of the pleasure in forming the collection was derived from her encounters with dealers and their wares in Bond Street and its environs. By this means she cultivated her eye for quality and for a bargain.

Mrs Gubbay's friendship with Queen Mary lasted until the Queen's death in 1953, and one of her gifts from the Queen is displayed in the Blue China Room. She was very close to the Duke and Duchess of York (later George VI and Queen Elizabeth the Queen Mother), advising them on the decoration and furnishing of 145 Piccadilly, and making baby clothes for Princess Elizabeth. Mrs Gubbay also advised Queen Mary's fourth son, Prince George, Duke of Kent, the only one of her children to share her artistic interests, and a collector on a grand scale, who has been described by Sir Oliver Millar as 'the most distinguished royal connoisseur since George IV'.

Mrs Gubbay not only lent to exhibitions, but also organised them. Her first recorded loans were to the Burlington Fine Arts Club's 1925 exhibition, and in 1928 she organised her first exhibition in collaboration with Sir Philip Sassoon. This was devoted to English secular needlework from the 15th century onwards, and several items from her own collection reflect her abiding interest in textiles, particularly in upholstery and carpets. Mrs Gubbay was an expert needlewoman, whose friendship with the Queen was inaugurated by their joint interest in the Needlework Guilds. This exhibition, like the ensuing annual shows at Park Lane, was a vast affair, involving hundreds of objects, the production of catalogues and all the complexities and paraphernalia of modern exhibitions.

In 1929 her exhibition of old English silver was, according to *Country Life*, 'amazing both in quantity and quality'. Mrs Gubbay lent a silver fruit dish inlaid with mother-of-pearl made in London in 1621 (none of her silver came to Clandon, having been sold by the National Trust to raise money for the upkeep of the rest of the collection). In 1920 the exhibition was of English conversation-pieces (Mrs Gubbay owned hardly any pictures), but in 1931 the *Four Georges* exhibition was of English Georgian furniture as well as pictures, and was followed by the *Age of Walnut*, returning to Mrs Gubbay's favourite early 18th century.

In 1934 the theme was porcelain. *Vogue*'s account indicated how well established these exhibitions had become:

At 25 Park Lane one passes the massed hyacinths with reluctance and mounts the white marble stairs, sees the first spring hats, greets the celebrities and does the tour, catalogue in hand…. A group of visitors surrounds Mrs Gubbay, who for years has organised this little miracle – an exhibition without a dull or ugly thing in it. 'No relics' is her wise rule!

Mrs Gubbay's own collection was well represented. Like Mrs Greville and other contemporary collectors, she had a catholic interest in English, continental and oriental porcelain. Perhaps the most extraordinary, and certainly the most striking, aspect of her collection of porcelain is the large flock of 17th- and 18th-century Chinese porcelain birds. As a set, they are unrivalled and are placed upon numerous rare mid-18th-century English giltwood brackets. Mrs Gubbay's avian enthusiasms apparently derived from her Indian childhood, and a favourite pet mynah bird. Her continental porcelain encompassed the production of most of

Two pieces from Mrs Gubbay's famous collection of Chinese porcelain birds

the famous factories, including Sèvres, Meissen, Nymphenburg and Tournai. She was particularly interested in Meissen figures, including many by the famous modeller J. J. Kaendler. She also compiled a large collection of English porcelain, mainly Bow, Chelsea and Derby, and of Staffordshire pottery.

Mrs Gubbay's husband, David (who was a first cousin), was responsible for managing Sir Philip Sassoon's branch of the family firm and his personal finances. David Gubbay was rich in his own right (his mother was a Rothschild), so there were ample funds for collecting. Asthmatic and overworked, he died in 1929, and Mrs Gubbay remained a widow until her death nearly 40 years later (there were no children).

In 1972 Frank Davis concluded his article on the new arrangements at Clandon as follows:

The donor I think would have been pleased if she could see how her beloved collection has been arranged. I can see her still, darting about in the Sassoon Park Lane mansion, bright of eye, arranging those annual exhibitions, a no-nonsense perfectionist if ever there was one. Not everyone loved her, but she mellowed with the years and the National Trust and through it all of us remain in her debt.

On receipt of the Gubbay bequest, the Trust acted quickly to link it with Clandon, whose redecoration by John Fowler was completed within three years, and which reopened, with the Gubbay collection installed, on 1 May 1971. The importation of a collection to be shown alongside the rump of what had been a much larger Onslow collection marked a departure from the Trust's usual practice of maintaining its houses 'as found'. The repair, redecoration and rearrangement of the house also radically changed the character of Clandon.

Before 1969, the state rooms remained – in terms of decoration, if not contents – much as they had been when last occupied by the Earls of Onslow. But there had been changes elsewhere. Already, between 1956 and 1966, the lead and slate valleyed roof had been replaced by a flat copper sheet, and the Marble Hall ceiling was supported from above by steel girders. In the process, the 'attic' rooms were rendered uninhabitable and their previously grand character – as family and guest bedrooms –

was irreversibly compromised. In the basement, visitor lavatories and other facilities were installed, and essential requirements (such as the provision of electrical plant), as well as the installation of the Queen's Royal Surrey Regiment Museum, obscured the original uses of most of the rooms (apart from the Kitchen, which was opened for the first time). The problem at Clandon in this regard is that there are no convenient outbuildings, as there are in most country houses. Most significant of course was the treatment of the principal rooms on the ground and first floors. At the time, this was probably the greatest transformation of a country house that the Trust had ever undertaken.

JOHN FOWLER

The major role was played by John Fowler (1906–77), who established his career as a decorator when he joined the Sybil Colefax partnership in 1938. By 1968 he was probably the most experienced country-house decorator of the day, and Clandon offered an exceptional opportunity to put his historical knowledge to practical use on behalf of an institutional rather than a traditional private client. It is clear that Fowler was given a very free hand by the Trust, and that his advice was not only sought – and usually taken – on the decorative front, but also in relation to the display of the Gubbay and Onslow collections. The main protagonist on the Trust's staff was St John Gore, who then combined the roles of regional Historic Buildings Representative and Adviser on Paintings. John Cornforth also offered advice and was co-author of the Trust's first guidebook to Clandon with Pamela, Countess of Onslow.

During the winter of 1967–8 – as Cornforth's 1969 *Country Life* articles reveal – Fowler, 'who had already done some work in the house, carried out test scrapes in the saloon'. Underneath the 'whitewash', his findings revealed an elaborate colour scheme that he took to be the original early 18th-century treatment of the room. We now know that this was an 1879 redecoration by the 4th Earl, but at the time 'this made the shortage of money all the more frustrating, and so the decision to display Mrs Gubbay's collection in the house was all the more

John Fowler removed the whitewash from the columns in the Marble Hall to reveal the 1870s marbling

welcome'. The money that came with the Gubbay collection, and the Levy family's grant, allowed the realisation of Fowler's plans, although there was never enough either for authentic replicas of textiles or to complete his proposals for the first floor.

Work started at the end of the 1968 open season, with the Marble Hall and Saloon as essential priorities, given the opportunity especially to reveal the supposedly early 18th-century treatment of the latter. Several years before, Fowler had cleaned off the whitewash from the lower order of the Marble Hall columns to 'reveal the original marbling', and this was now extended to the skirting and base blocks of the columns. Again, this marbling is now known to be of the 1870s. In the Saloon, Fowler found that the whitewash of the ceiling could simply be washed off, revealing the previous colours that he thought were early 18th-century, although the walls 'could not be cleaned' and he left scrapes to show visitors how closely the colours had been matched. This was pioneering work – heralding a conservative approach to historic decoration subsequently adopted by the Trust – but it was (as we now know) based on a false premise, that the decoration was early 18th-century rather than Victorian. John Harris and James Lees-Milne suspected the truth at the time, the latter describing it in 1973 as 'the most hideous decoration I had seen: flesh pink (which John Fowler calls biscuit) and purple [*sic*]'.

John Cornforth described Fowler's approach as 'empirical,... influenced by such a variety of considerations, visual and comparative evidence, historical style and sentiment, the need to create a unity where there may be elements of different dates to be absorbed, the limitations imposed by money and so on'. The primary aim, however, was to be true to the early 18th-century origins of Clandon, and to reveal what was thought to be most authentic. Sometimes, quite radical measures were taken to achieve this. In the Green Drawing Room, what is now thought to have been the pre-1778 *brocatelle* was removed from the walls to reveal the original green paper beneath. In the State Bedroom, the 1740s chimneypiece was removed and replaced by an earlier chimneypiece from an upstairs bedroom (this was on the assumption that the 1740s chimneypiece was moved there in the 19th century). In the Stone Staircase, early 19th-century graining – presumably applied when the Speakers' Parlour was redecorated by the 1st Earl – was overpainted on the doorcases and dado in a reversion to stone colour. In the Speakers' Parlour itself, a large section of the graining on the cornice was removed to reveal the 1720s treatment of the room, despite the previously untouched survival of the 1st Earl's grained and gilded scheme. Upstairs, in the so-called State Dining Room, 19th-century partitions were taken down to restore the original proportions, but although it was known that the room had been hung with green flock wallpaper, it was painted 'broken yellow', chosen to complement the Barlow fowl paintings, which were moved here from the Stone Staircase.

Even the principal rooms had their decoration modified – the 1720s ceilings (originally plain white) had colour added to tie up with other elements of the rooms (blue in the Palladio Room, green in the Green Drawing Room). Other similar modifications were made in the cause of style, and whole interiors were redecorated without historical precedent (the Oak Stairs and Marble Hall Gallery, the 'Blue China Room', the Hunting Room and the Morning Room). Curtains, carpets and upholstery were also supplied that were not based on what had gone before (eg in the Hunting and Morning Rooms). Fowler's decision to reupholster the seat furniture of the Palladio Room (red on the chairs, yellow on the sofas) was intended to 'link the curtains and wallpaper together by complementing them' – an entirely modern decorator's concept.

This dichotomy between traditional and contemporary practice is at the heart of John Fowler's treatment of Clandon, and is the aspect of his work that provokes most unease today. However, it needs to be understood that the restoration of Clandon was undertaken at a time around 1970, when the Trust and other institutions such as the V & A, were beginning to develop a more thorough approach to historical decoration based on preliminary archival and technical research (such as 'scrapes' and paint analysis). Previously, it was enough to hire a decorator – preferably a fashionable one – to work with a client, but essentially to put his or her stamp upon a house. It is greatly to Fowler's and the Trust's credit that John Cornforth's *Country Life* articles explained what had been done, by addressing both the opportunities and the constraints. As our knowledge develops – and this guidebook is a product of continuing research – it is increasingly possible to identify shortcomings in what has gone before. It would be wrong therefore to judge Fowler's work at Clandon with the benefit of hindsight, without an attempt to put it in context. It was pioneering and brave to undertake the renaissance of a sparsely furnished house where previously there had been a marked contrast between its grandeur and 'its failure to impress visitors'. Fowler's work is in itself a landmark in the history of late 20th-century country-house decoration, and his contribution to Clandon needs to be seen as that of an historically minded decorator on the brink of a new era of country-house curatorship.

BIBLIOGRAPHY

Manuscript sources

The Onslow family papers are owned by Lord Onslow and are on deposit in the Surrey History Centre, Woking. The majority of the surviving papers date from the 1870s and the inheritance of the 4th Earl of Onslow. There are some earlier papers in the collection; these are mostly Wills and Deeds. The 4th Earl of Onslow's garden diaries and notebooks, and the 4th Countess's guest and menu books, are in the Library at Clandon.

ALLEN, Thomas, *A New and Complete History of the Counties of Surrey and Sussex*, ii, London, 1829.

AVERY, Tracey, 'Four Georges: The Decorative Art Collections of Mrs David Gubbay and Lady Binning', *Apollo*, April 1999, pp. 16–19.

BRAYLEY, E.W., *History of Surrey,* v, London, 1850.

CORNFORTH, John, 'Clandon Revisited', *Country Life,* 4, 11 December 1969, pp. 1456–60, 1582–6.

CORNFORTH, John and Gervase Jackson-Stops, 'The Gubbay Collection at Clandon Park', *Country Life,* 29 April 1971, p. 1004f.

CURTIS, Charles, 'Clandon Park', *The Gardeners' Magazine,* 6 May 1911, pp. 341–3.

DAVIS, Frank, 'The Gubbay bequest at Clandon Park', *Antique Collector,* December 1972, pp. 312–15.

DAVIS, Frank, 'Mrs David Gubbay's Collection of Mirrors', *Country Life,* 15 February 1930.

FOWLER, John and John Cornforth, *English Decoration in the 18th Century*, London, 1978.

GALLOP, Alan, *The House with the Golden Eyes*, Sunbury-on-Thames, 1998.

Gardeners' Chronicle, 'Clandon Park', 5 December 1885, p. 712.

Gardeners' Chronicle, 'Clandon Park', 13 August 1910, pp. 113–15.

HEWLINGS, Richard, 'James Leoni *c.*1689–1746', *Architectural Outsiders*, London, 1985.

Historical Manuscripts Commission, *Fourteenth Report Appendix Part IX. The Manuscripts of the Earl of Buckinghamshire … the Earl of Onslow …*, London, 1895.

JACKSON, Stanley, *The Sassoons: Portrait of a Dynasty*, London, 1989.

MANNING, James, *The Lives of the Speakers of the House of Commons*, London, 1850.

MOORE, Andrew ed., *Houghton Hall*, London, 1994.

ONSLOW, 5th Earl of, *Sixty-three Years*, London, 1944.

ONSLOW, 6th Earl of, *Men and Sand*, London, 1961.

ONSLOW, Pamela, 'A House that was once a Home', *Vogue,* 1971, pp. 64–74.

SUPPLE, Barry, *The Royal Exchange Assurance: A History of British Insurance 1720–1970,* Cambridge, 1970.

TIPPING, H. Avray, 'Clandon Park, Surrey', *Country Life,* 10, 17, 24 September 1927, pp. 366–72, 398–404, 434–40.

VULLIAMY, C.E., *The Onslow Family 1528–1874*, London, 1953.

WHELDALE, Muriel, *Huia Onslow*, London, 1933.